The Complete Guide
to
Single-Engine Cessnas

4th Edition

Joe Christy
Revised and updated by Brian J. Dooley

TAB Books
Division of McGraw-Hill, Inc.
Blue Ridge Summit, PA 17294-0850

FOURTH EDITION
THIRD PRINTING

© 1993 by **TAB Books.**
TAB Books is a division of McGraw-Hill, Inc.

Library of Congress Cataloging-in-Publication Data

Christy, Joe.
   The complete guide to single-engine Cessnas / by Joe Christy ;
revised and updated by Brian J. Dooley. — 4th ed.
      p.   cm.
   Includes index.
   ISBN 0-8306-4224-2
   1. Cessna (Airplanes) I. Dooley, Brian J. II. Title.
TL686.C4C45 1992
629.133'343—dc20   92-29913
                                                CIP

Acquisitions Editor: Jeff Worsinger
Editor: Norval G. Kennedy
Director of Production: Katherine G. Brown
Book Design: Jaclyn J. Boone
Cover Design: Holberg Design, York, PA   AV1
Cover Photograph: Courtesy of Cessna Aircraft Company   4274

Contents

Acknowledgments

MANY THANKS to all of those who contributed to this volume. In particular, I would like to single out the contributions of the Nierenbergs, owner/operators of Princeton Airport, for helping out with information and photos in the midst of a barrage of airport-saving activity. I would also like to thank Cessna Aircraft, now a part of Textron, for helping out in the midst of a move to new facilities. Then, there are individual contributions, such as that of my friend Shiddhartha Sangal who let us play cat and mouse with his Cardinal RG over Round Valley in search of the perfect photograph, and Robert Slobins, who helped out with some of the photography. While I cannot mention everyone here, I thank you all for your contributions.

Introduction

CLYDE VERNON CESSNA was a 31-year-old automobile mechanic in 1910 when he saw a trio of magnificent men perform in their flying machines at Oklahoma City. Clyde made detailed sketches of the Bleriot monoplane possessed by one of the birdmen and, a year later, had built a passable replica, which he flew at the Salt Plains near Jet, Oklahoma, after 12 attempts and 11 crashes. Clyde thereupon forsook the horseless carriage business and embarked upon an aerial exhibition tour of the county fair circuit. His first appearance was at Cherokee, Oklahoma, for which he received $300 for simply taking off and circling the pasture. Such an accomplishment, in 1911, was unquestionably worth every cent of it.

During the next six years, until World War I intervened, Cessna became a highly successful exhibition pilot, which was the only way there was to make a living with an airplane in those days. He built an improved craft each winter at the family farm near Rago, Kansas. By 1917, his Comet monoplane averaged 124.62 mph in a flight between Wichita, Kansas, and Blackwell, Oklahoma.

Clyde was 37 years old when America entered World War I and was not accepted for military service. He farmed until 1919, then returned to the air. Late in 1924, he was still barnstorming, flying a Laird Swallow—sold to him by a Swallow salesman named Walter Herschel Beech. Walter Beech and another Swallow employee, Lloyd Carlton Stearman, talked Cessna into joining them in the formation of a new airplane manufacturing business. With $10,000 in capital put up by Beech and Cessna, and Stearman's drawings of a three-place biplane, the Travel Air Company began operation with six employees in a small shop behind the Broadview Hotel in downtown Wichita.

But three chiefs in a single tepee made at least two too many. Though Travel Air grew rapidly, Stearman pulled out in 1926 to form his own company (later absorbed by Boeing), and Cessna sold out the following year to found the Cessna

Clyde Cessna and a 1917 Cessna aircraft.

Aircraft Company (after several months as the Cessna-Roos Aircraft Corporation in partnership with Victor H. Roos, a former associate of Giuseppe M. Bellanca). Beech continued successfully with Travel Air, which was merged into the then giant Curtiss-Wright complex in 1929.

Meanwhile, Cessna steadily built his company. In 1929, he purchased 80 acres at Cessna's present main plant site and constructed five buildings. He had 80 employees, and his products were the Cessna Model A series: clean, four-place cantilever monoplanes powered with a variety of engines, the most popular of which was the Model AW, fitted with a 125-hp Warner or a 200-hp Wright Whirlwind. These Cessnas were Clyde's own designs, and were so basically sound one can still see some Model AWs in single-engine Cessnas today. Between 1931 and 1936, Cessnas won the Detroit News "World's Most Efficient Airplane" trophy three times to gain permanent possession of that famed award.

The Great Depression halted production at Cessna in 1932, and one can only speculate as to what might have happened to the company (Clyde was nearing retirement age, and other airframe makers were being liquidated almost daily as the economic disaster worsened) had not Clyde given an airplane ride to his 12-year-old nephew, Dwane L. Wallace, back in 1923. From that time forward, young Wallace knew that his future would be in aviation. He soloed an OX-5 Travel Air in 1932 and graduated from Wichita State University in 1933 with a bachelor's degree in aeronautical engineering.

Because Cessna was closed down, Dwane worked briefly for Walter Beech (who had started Beech Aircraft Corporation in 1932, offering the Model 17 Staggerwing), then Dwane persuaded his uncle to reorganize the Cessna Aircraft Company and reopen the plant, producing a new four- to five-place monoplane of outstanding performance. The resulting Cessna Airmaster kept the company alive and is regarded as a classical design today.

Clyde retired to his farm in 1936 (he died in 1954), and Dwane Wallace, at age

L-19 Bird Dog
Aviation Hall of Fame of New Jersey

25, became president of the company, as well as part-time janitor, test pilot, engineer, and chief salesman. Prize money won by Wallace racing the new C-34 Airmaster usually went to meet the company's modest payroll. Production averaged fewer than 30 units per year for 1934 through 1938.

The coming aircraft production demands of World War II signaled an abrupt change in Cessna's fortunes. The company's first twin-engine plane, the T-50, appeared in 1939 and was bought first by the RCAF, then by the USAAF. More than 5,400 of these craft were built during World War II as the AT-8, AT-17, and UC-78. The British and Canadians called it the "Crane"; the USAAF designation was "Bobcat." But to the cadets who transitioned in this twin-engine trainer, it was affectionately, if irreverently, known as the "Useless-78," "Bamboo Bomber," or "Rhapsody in Glue."

Also during World War II, Cessna produced troop-carrying gliders, and sub-assemblies for Boeing and Douglas with greatly expanded factory facilities.

When the war ended, the company again turned to the commercial aircraft business. After a five-month conversion, Cessna introduced its first postwar models, the two-place 120 and 140. Production of these neat little craft reached 30 units per day in the summer of 1946, and that year's sales totaled nearly 4,000 airplanes.

Cessna broadened its market in 1947 with introduction of the four-place 190 and 195, essentially, all-metal Airmasters. And the following year production was started on the new four-place Model 170.

The L-19 Bird Dog (later designated O-1 by the Army) appeared in 1949, then the Korean War claimed a large portion of Cessna's production capacity with sub-assemblies for Boeing, Lockheed, and Republic. But in 1954, along with the T-37 jet trainer, the five-place twin-engine Model 310 was introduced to the public. The tricycle-gear Models 172 and 182 came out in 1955, and then, when the two-place tri-gear Model 150 was added in 1959, the basic Cessna line of single-engine aircraft was established for years to come.

That was the year that Cessna expanded into the electronics business with acquisition of Aircraft Radio Corporation (ARC), and the year that total company sales for the first time passed the $100 million mark. In 1969, total sales were $282.9 million. And it is probably worth remarking that, in 1939 when Dwane Wallace closed the deal with Canada for the first 180 Cranes, there was exactly $5.03 in the company's bank account.

In 1985, Cessna was merged with General Dynamics Corp., and in 1992, Cessna was sold to Textron for $600 million in cash. Although the company had been doing well with its Citation jet and Caravan turboprop business, it was overshadowed by the multibillion dollar General Dynamics defense business. In 1990, Cessna sold $716 million worth of airplanes and made $106 million. Because Textron also owns Lycoming engines and Bell Helicopters, this puts Cessna in interesting company.

This bit of good news, unfortunately, comes in the midst of increasingly dismal news from the light plane market. In 1986, Cessna quit the business entirely, focusing only upon its turboprop Caravan and jet Citation lines. Piper is sold, and probably won't manufacture single engine aircraft in the U.S. again. Beech, Mooney, and others have done some business, but it is not substantial. Inflation, an enormous fleet of available used planes, and mounting liability insurance costs have all played their part in virtually destroying the profitability of small planes.

In this book, you will see the incredible changes in pricing. Bear in mind that all of these aircraft, even the 140s and 120s, are still very much with us. If automobiles had undergone a similar evolution, most cars on the road would have fins, used cars would sell for their original retail price, and new economy models would cost more than a Porsche.

The used aircraft prices in this book come from the *Aircraft Bluebook Price Digest*, Fall 1991, published by Intertec Publishing Corporation, and edited by Fletcher Aldredge; it is the principal source used by dealers for valuation, first published in 1952.

Specifications and aircraft diagrams come from Cessna Aircraft Company's aircraft manuals and are reprinted with permission. Aircraft performance and specification figures are for illustration purposes only; the figures are not to be used in the actual operation of aircraft.

1

Cessna 120 and 140

IN 1992, WE CHECKED WITH THE INTERNATIONAL CESSNA 120/140 Association to see just what was happening at this end of the market; many are still around. Bill Rhoades from the association reported on current registrations: 991 120s; 2,377 140s; and 297 120As. Though not all these are flyable aircraft, it still represents a substantial collection.

The 120s and 140s are still fairly popular as used aircraft, though their place as cheap entry-level planes has been largely usurped by older 150s. Still, 120s and 140s are attractively priced, have performance characteristics that compare favorably with 150s, and have developed a strong following within the taildragger crowd.

The fabric-wing 140, which sold for a maximum of $3,495 new (1946–49), was bringing from $2,000 to $2,400, 25 years later. Inflation and market conditions have taken the price of this same plane (given a good restoration) all the way to $10,000, 40 years later in 1992. A good metal-wing 140A or a 140 with metalized wing that had an original list price of $3,695, was commanding up to $2,750 in the 1970 market and $10,000 in 1992.

In addition to inflation, market conditions, and all of the factors that have recently affected light plane sales, the basic soundness of the early postwar Cessnas contributes to their high resale value. The 120/140 is a trim little ship with honest flying characteristics and performance matching or exceeding that of the later 150.

The 120 and 140 are basically the same airplane; the 120 being the economy version without electrical system, starter or flaps, and possessing a minimum of instruments. Both aircraft are powered with the C-85 Continental engine, except for the 521 metal-winged 140As produced at the factory, which were fitted with a Continental C-90. Because many fabric-wing 140s were later converted to metal-wingers, these will probably still be equipped with the 85-hp engine and therefore are not 140As. As originally delivered from Cessna, all 120s and 140s were unpainted, except of course for silver dope finish on the fabric wings. In recent years, however, many have been given modern paint schemes.

Some 120s have been fitted with the Continental C-85-12 (the 140 engine, which has starter and generator) and a complete electrical system; and though such a craft might be called a 140, it really isn't, unless it has also been given the

Cessna 140

140's wings with flaps and the 140's plusher cabin and extra instruments. But it does come close, because the 140's flaps are not the big para-lift barn-door airfoils found on later Cessnas, and do not help much, if any, on short takeoffs, and though useful for landings, will seem anemic if you've been flying, say, a 150.

For comparison purposes, at the end of the '60s, there were about 1,200 120s and 3,500 140s still around.

FLIGHT FAMILIARIZATION

Entering the 140 will at first seem an awkward and ungraceful exercise to those unaccustomed to the older tail-draggers, but it's no worse than a T-Craft, Luscombe, or Aeronca, and it certainly beats boarding a J-3 Cub. The seats are comfortable, but the cabin is small and becomes cramped for two (sitting side-by-side) if both are more than 175 pounds.

Starter, throttle, parking brake, carburetor heat, and mixture control are at bottom center of the instrument panel, with electrical switches immediately beneath. Elevator trim, flap control, and fuel selector switch are between the seats. The fuel selector switch is three-position, for either of the two 12½-gallon wing tanks, or "Off." Fuel gauges are of the direct-reading type and located in each wing root inside the cabin. Fuel to the engine is gravity-fed via the selector-switch junction, then through a strainer on the firewall to the carburetor.

These little Continental engines are easy to start (when properly maintained), though on a cold day three or four strokes of the primer are required. Because this is a tailwheel airplane, taxi in an S-pattern to clear the blind spot over the nose. During the pretakeoff check, test mags at 1,800 rpms; set carb heat at "Cold," turn elevator trim wheel to "Takeoff"; determine that flaps are up and locked, and, of course, be sure the fuel selector is turned to the fullest tank. This is also when you are supposed to lock the door and windows, although we can't guarantee that they'll stay that way on some 140s after all these years.

Cessna 140 on floats

PERFORMANCE

Average takeoff roll with the 140 at full gross load (1,450 lbs) is between 600 and 750 feet in a no-wind condition, depending upon ground elevation and temperature. Holding the tail a little below horizontal, she breaks ground at slightly faster than 40 mph. Then, climb-out should be made at between 80–90 mph for good engine cooling. This will give you a rate-of-climb of about 600 feet per minute initially, and on a normal day, somewhere between 300 and 400 fpm at 7,000 ft.

Sure, this is less than fighter airplane performance, but you are aviating with 85 horsepower and burning only 5 gallons of gasoline per hour. At the 140's normal cruising speed of 105 mph, that's more than 20 miles per gallon. Full throttle (2,575 rpms), will up your speed to between 115–120 mph and raise gas consumption to about 6 gallons per hour.

Stalls are gentle in the 120 and 140. We once read a pilot report in an aviation magazine wherein the writer said the 140 "stalls without warning." He just wasn't payin' attention. This craft does have a marked buffet preceding the stall. The nose falls through at about 47 mph, power off and clean. With flaps and power off, the break comes at about 43 or 44 mph. Flaps down and power on, she quits flying at about 38 mph. Recovery is quick, and there is some aileron control into the stall, although the 140's ailerons, like those on other single-engine Cessnas, are a bit too soft to suit some pilots.

Landing the 140, use carburetor heat and set the mixture control at "Full Rich." Sixty-five to seventy mph is a good gliding speed, with some nose-up trim cranked in to lighten the control pressure. Flaps will steepen your glide without a build-up in airspeed, and do help to sink through the ground cushion after flare-

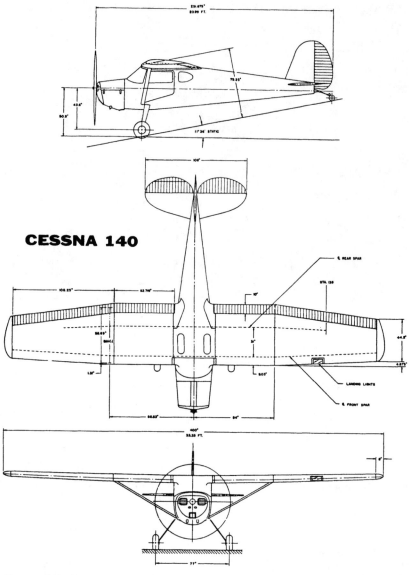

CESSNA 140

Cessna 140 views

out. The 120, which has no flaps, seems to want to float a little at this point. But both 120 and 140 are fairly easy to land, and each has a relatively wide tread for planes of this configuration (the first of the Cessna steel-spring landing gears), and therefore are surefooted on the ground.

WHAT TO LOOK FOR

In sum, a 120 or 140 represents a reasonable low-end buy—assuming that you find one that has been well maintained and isn't on the brink of expensive refurbishing.

One FAA bulletin (AD note) of consequence issued on these planes was AD50-31-1, which calls for a reinforcement to the vertical fin spar. So, if you're thinking of buying such a plane, check the airframe log to make sure this has been complied with.

You'll also want to make a close inspection for corrosion and determine the condition of the wing fabric, among other things. But let's face it, there is really only one reasonably safe way to select a used airplane of any kind; hire an experienced A&P mechanic who has no interest in the deal one way or another to thoroughly inspect a plane before you buy it.

Yes, it might hurt a little to ante up the money for the inspection, particularly if you go home without that airplane you had your heart set on, but it's better than buying a machine that spends much of its time in the shop running up repair bills.

Bill Rhoades of the 120/140 Association notes, "We have members that have installed the Continental O-200 [most popular installation], the Lycoming O-235, O-290, and O-290D2 engines in their planes. I have seen two installations of the Lycoming 150-hp O-320 and there are rumors that someone installed the 160-hp Lycoming with a constant-speed propeller.

"Other modifications include 60 amp alternator (replacing the 10A generator), Cessna 150 seats, Cessna 150 exhaust, lifting handles below the leading edge of the horizontal stabilizer, Cessna 150 instrument panel with center stack radios, and wing leading edge lights. There were several STCs adding metal to the wings of the 120 and 140. Unusual modifications include a [jet-assisted takeoff] JATO system and an agricultural sprayer system mounted under the wings."

Table 1-1. Cessna 140 performance & specifications.

Takeoff Distance	500 ft
Rate-of-climb (Initial)	680 ft per min
Service Ceiling	15,500 ft
Top Speed	125 mph
Cruising Speed	105 mph
Range (*with reserve)	450 mi
Stall Speed (without power; flaps up)	49 mph
Stall Speed (without power; flaps down)	45 mph
Landing Roll (without brakes)	230 ft
Engine	Continental C-85 or C-90
Wing Span	33 ft 4 in
Length	21 ft 6 in
Height	6 ft 3 in
Wing Area	159.3 sq ft
Wing Loading	9.1 lbs sq ft
Power Loading	17.1 lbs per hp
Empty Weight	120, 770; 140, 890 lb
Gross Weight	1,450 lbs
Useful Load	120, 680; 140, 560 lb
Fuel Capacity	25 gal
Oil Capacity	5 qts

Original factory figures computed at full gross load and standard atmosphere (sea level; 59 degrees F).

2

Cessna 190 and 195

OUR DESCRIPTION of the Cessna 190 and 195 will undoubtedly be a little biased, but it's not our fault. We don't start feuds with airplanes or other inanimate objects. But "Shakey Jake" clearly disliked us from the beginning. Shakey was a 195 who belonged to a flying club. He got his name from his Jacobs engine, and he was brought to us for sundry maintenance and repairs. That is, he was brought to our shops when we were in the FBO business several years ago.

Shakey was in and out of our place for many months, during which time he humiliated this writer on many occasions, dripped oil on our clean floors and obviously would have done us bodily harm had he ever gotten the chance. He had a crosswind landing gear, and every time he saw us approach him he'd splay his wheels in different directions and dare us to move him. Everyone else around there could roll Shakey to or from the hangars and he'd go quietly. But not for this reporter; he hated us.

Shakey got the best of us in the end. His owners brought him in for a new windshield and, innocently, we gave an estimate and agreed to do the job. Well, please be advised, friends, such a request should be regarded in law as sufficient provocation for justifiable homicide. At least, when it involves an airplane with Shakey's delinquent social tendencies.

As it happened, our AI was away on a ferry flight, our number one A&P was on vacation, and there was no one in the shops except a young A&P just out of vo-tech school. And it quickly became apparent that replacing a 195 windshield was a job for two skilled airframe mechanics. But, naturally, Shakey would not have needed a windshield had our experienced men been on hand. Also, as you would expect, this happened in the middle of an Oklahoma summer. So, we sat in Shakey's cabin—where the temperature approximated that of Death Valley—for a couple of days, and tried to guess which of the roughly 4,000 locknuts we were supposed to hold while the young A&P tightened from the outside and the suspicion grew that our replacement windshield was really for a DC-3 or something else. Anyway, our AI returned at the end of the week, looked at the job in amazement, and did it all over again. We probably only lost a few hundred dollars on the deal.

1953 Cessna 195

With this as background, you'll understand if we are less than enthusiastic about the 195. As we said at the start, it clearly isn't our fault. Any pilot will agree that some airplanes just naturally dislike some people.

ON THE MARKET

The first 190 appeared in 1947 and was powered with the Continental R-670-23 engine of 240 hp. The 195 quickly followed, and was offered with a choice of three Jacobs powerplants: the 245-hp R-755-9; the 275-hp R-755-B2, and the 300-hp R-755-A2.

A total of 204 190s were built, 1947–1953 inclusive; and 890 195s were produced, 1947–1957 inclusive. In addition, 83 of the 300-hp 195s were built for the military as the LC-126, 1950-1952, with 15 going to the Air Force, 5 to the Air National Guard and 63 to the Army (our nemesis, Shakey, was actually an Army surplus LC-126).

Prices ranged from $12,750 for early models up to $24,700 for the last 300-hp 195s. About 450 Cessna 195s were still on the FAA's "active" list in 1970; and some could be found on the used airplane market for $6,000 to $7,000 in "average" condition. It should be noted, however, that this craft possesses an impressive number of staunch friends, enough to form an International 195 Club, and these owners, flying mint-condition 195s, do not of course place "average" prices on them—if and when they are willing to sell at all. Thus, there were some like-new (or better-than-new) 195s around, valued from $10,000 upwards at the beginning of the seventies.

Prices have continued to rise rather sharply for the 195s, slightly ahead of the normal curve for no-longer-manufactured general aviation aircraft. A typical selling price in the 1990s is $35,000.

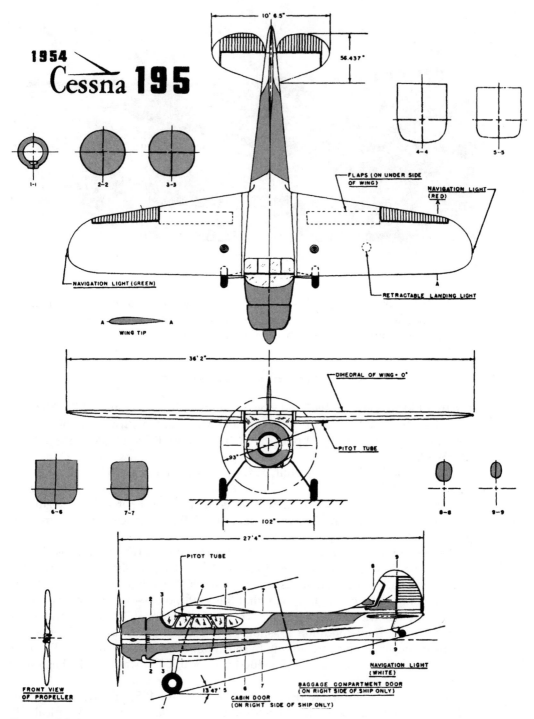

1954 _Cessna_ **195**

10' 6.5"

56.437"

4—4

5—5

1—1

2—2

3—3

FLAPS (ON UNDER SIDE OF WING)

NAVIGATION LIGHT (RED)

NAVIGATION LIGHT (GREEN)

RETRACTABLE LANDING LIGHT

A

WING TIP

36' 2"

DIHEDRAL OF WING = 0°

PITOT TUBE

.93"

6—6

7—7

8—8

9—9

102"

27' 4"

PITOT TUBE

NAVIGATION LIGHT (WHITE)

13'47' 5

BAGGAGE COMPARTMENT DOOR (ON RIGHT SIDE OF SHIP ONLY)

CABIN DOOR (ON RIGHT SIDE OF SHIP ONLY)

FRONT VIEW OF PROPELLER

Cessna 195 views

S-TURN TAXI REQUIRED

Most 195s have a retracting step that extends when the cabin door is opened; on some this step might be permanently fixed. The cabin is roomy—positively spacious by lightplane standards—with a pair of individual adjustable seats in front and a solid-cushion type seat in back that accommodates three. As is obvious from the outside, forward visibility over the nose, from the pilots' seats, is very limited when this airplane is in three-point attitude. While on the ground, an acre or two of instrument panel seems to block out most of the world, so taxiing must be done in an S-pattern if you want a clue as to what you're about to run into.

Fuel from the 40-gallon tank in each wing (total: 80 gal.) is gravity-fed to the Continental engine in the 190, but a fuel pump is used in the 195 because of its higher horsepower. In case of fuel-pump failure, a by-pass line will keep the Jacobs supplied with sufficient fuel by gravity alone to maintain normal cruise. The Jacobs must be primed on every start; two or three strokes of the primer on warm days and five to seven strokes on cold days.

FLIGHT FAMILIARIZATION

Starting the Jacobs, fuel mixture of course is set at "Full Rich"; carburetor heat at "Cold," but the propeller is set at "Low RPM" to prevent taking too much oil from the engine at this point. With the master switch "On," the engine primed and throttle cracked, turn the key ignition to "Battery Start" position, make sure your prop is clear and then press the starter button. As soon as the engine fires, turn the key ignition to "Both Run." The engine may require another shot or two of prime to keep it running at first.

By this time, the roomy transport-type cabin, generous expanse of instrument panel and that big radial barking defiance at the world, might combine to give you the air of Captain Sternjaw, departing upon his regular run to Kalamazoo. If so, okay, because there are times when this airplane needs full attention and a bit of professionalism in flying technique, especially after landing flareout in a crosswind, when it has a strong tendency to weathercock.

During the takeoff run, visibility over the nose improves as the tail comes up. Full right rudder trim will compensate for much of the torque, and the 195 will fly off at about 60 mph—with an average takeoff roll of about 900 feet—in a slightly tail-low attitude.

Full throttle is allowable for one minute, and this will give you an initial climb rate of about 1,000 fpm at 2,200 rpms and 85 mph. But the recommended climb/cruise configuration is 2,000 rpms at 23 inches of manifold pressure with about 100 knots or 115 mph showing. This produces, usually, around 500 to 600 fpm, and the 195 will hold this, with very little drop in the rate-of-climb, through 4,000 feet.

Although a lot of people have described the 195 as a "good instrument airplane," we'd have to disagree. True, good turns (without altitude loss or gain) are easier on instruments until one learns where the horizon should be with relation to the top of the instrument panel, or whatever you finally pick as a reference for eyeball turns, and because aileron response is slow, there's naturally less overcontrolling with a set of "white knuckles" on the wheel during instrument flight. The 195 does have a big airplane feel, which alone must induce a certain feeling of security. But it needs to be flown. In cruise configuration, no matter how carefully you trim it, the plane will, left to itself, slowly porpoise, alternately gaining and losing up to 75 feet or even more.

Stall behavior is neither good nor bad. The 195 has plenty of aileron into the stall, and you'll use it. Power off and clean, the stall comes at about 65 mph. With power off and flaps, the break is a bit sharper at about 62 mph. With power on and flaps down, the pay-off registers at about 56–58 mph. These figures are average, for a moderate day and at near full gross load.

CROSSWIND CORRECTION

This airplane is easy to land, if the wind is straight down the runway. In a crosswind, some artful rudder work is required and, as far as we were ever able to discover, a certain amount of good luck.

This trait undoubtedly prompted installation of a crosswind landing gear on some 195s (and 170s). And we'll say this for the crosswind gear: it does exactly what it's supposed to do. That is, it keeps you rolling straight down the runway while the airplane points in another direction. But it does take a modicum of faith to use it at first. Every nerve in your being will rebel at the prospect of actually touching-down while still crabbing 15 degrees or so into the wind. After a few landings, however, you'll probably feel it's the only practical gear for the 195. That is, until you have to wrestle the stubborn thing in and out of the hangar a few times.

Depending upon its condition, the 195 should give you a true air speed of 165–170 mph at 7,000 feet where about 70 percent of its power is available. Fuel consumption is about 16 gallons per hour with the 300-hp Jacobs.

ADs for 190s and 195s include a periodic requirement to x-ray the wing spar for hairline cracks, a need to inspect and/or repair seat rails, and a fuel cell inspection (12-month) plus a quick drain requirement.

Like we said in the beginning, this isn't a very objective report—maybe even a little unfair. But if an airplane ever gets it in for you, the way Shakey did for us, you'll understand.

Table 2-1. Cessna 195
performance & specifications.

Takeoff Distance	800 ft
Takeoff over 50-ft Obstacle	1,600 ft
Landing Distance	700 ft
Landing over 50-ft Obstacle	1,600 ft
Rate of Climb, Maximum Initial	1,200 ft per min
Service Ceiling	18,300 ft
Maximum Speed	185 mph
Cruise Speed (70% Power)	170 mph
Range at 70% Power	800 mi
Stall Speed, Power Off, Flaps 45 Degrees	62 mph
Engine	Jacobs R-755
Propeller	Hamilton Standard Constant Speed
Wing Span	36 ft 2 in
Length	27 ft 4 in
Height	7 ft 2 in
Wing Loading	15.36 lbs per sq ft
Power Loading	11.16 lbs per hp
Empty Weight	2,100 lbs
Gross Weight	3,350 lbs
Useful Load	1,250 lbs
Baggage Capacity	220 lbs
Fuel Capacity (usable)	75 gal
Oil Capacity	5 gal

3

Cessna 170

THE CESSNA 170 SERIES AIRPLANES are still in demand on the used market, more than 40 years after this design first appeared. Good ones, properly restored, were bringing 200 percent of their original purchase price in 1992. New prices ranged from $7,245 to $8,295 during production (1948–1955 inclusive), and a 170A or 170B in good condition would quickly find a buyer willing to pay up to $17,000 for it in 1992.

As with the used 140s, the Cessna 170 series compares very favorably, performance-wise, with the posher and sleeker tricycle gear models that replaced them. A comparison with the 1985 Model 172 (averaging $62,000 on the used market), will show what we mean:

	170B (1952)	172 Skyhawk (1985)
Top Speed	140 mph	141 mph
Cruising Speed	120 mph	138 mph
	(65% power)	(75% power)
Initial Climb Rate	690 fpm	700 fpm
Useful Load	995 lbs	974 lbs
Range	540 mi	440 nm

To be fair, we must point out that the above figures do not reflect the 172's added comfort, quieter cabin, easier landing and ground handling, 360-degree vision and a number of other little niceties, including a rakishly-swept rudder (which adds nothing except looks, and probably even costs a couple of mph in speed). And considering the additional fact that the 172 is considerably newer, while the 170B might have 6,000 hours or more on its aging frame, the newer 172 is generally a better buy at more than four times the price (including avionics)—if one has the money and/or a sound financial reason for operating a plane in this class.

But for the pilot who wants a four-placer primarily for pleasure, and cannot or does not wish to invest more than $17,000 in such a machine, a well-maintained 170 might well be a reasonable choice. It is also an excellent machine for the antique and restoration buff. If you consider the 170, you should also consider the possibility of an older 172, which is covered in a subsequent chapter.

1957 C-170B

MORE THAN 5,100 BUILT

The original 170 had a fabric-covered wing, two wing struts on each side, and a 140-type rudder. The 170A, which appeared in 1949, had a metal-covered wing and new dorsal fin, plus a single lift strut on each side. The 170B, similar to the 170A, but with L-19 type flaps added, was introduced in 1952. Officially, production ceased with the 1955 Model 170B; but 72 were built in 1956 (alongside the new 172), and 36 were produced in 1957, according to Cessna records. Altogether, 5,136 of the 170 series were built, and about 2,800 remained on the FAA's active list at the end of 1970.

The 170 is fairly easy to board for a tailwheel airplane and visibility over the nose is good. Noise-level in flight is about what you'd expect in an older airplane. This craft does want to weathercock on the ground in a good wind, and that can be a problem on a big airport when you have a long way to taxi. Having said that, it's hard to find any other fault with the 170. Its flying characteristics are all good; it's a pleasure to fly.

Following standard pretakeoff procedures, the 170B will normally become airborne in about 700–800 feet, depending upon weight and air density, indicating around 55 mph. Initial climb will be in the neighborhood of 700 fpm; up to 1,000 fpm if you are light.

FEWER MECHANICAL PROBLEMS

This is a stable airplane in all axes, and requires reasonable coordination between wheel and rudder pedals for good turns. The 170's 145-hp Continental engine delivers 65 percent power at 5,000 feet pressure altitude turning 2,450 rpms, and produces 120 mph TAS with 8 gph fuel consumption at this setting. Because later model Cessnas equipped with a similar engine cruise at 2,700 rpms, the 170's recommended cruise rpms should result in fewer mechanical problems.

Stalls are gentle in this craft, and there is no wing drop except in full-power

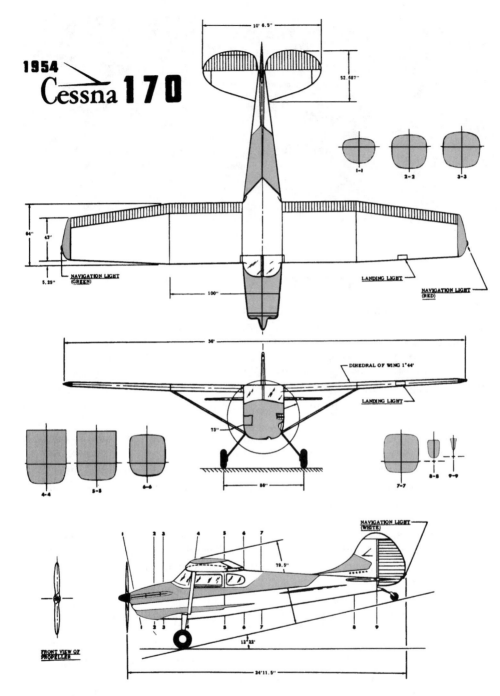

1954 C-170 views

stalls. In all cases, this machine recovers from the stall very quickly. We also regard the 170 as easy to land for a tail-dragger. It will float if you're carrying only a little too much speed; it was designed for full-stall landings. Still, the old pros tell us that's the way all lightplanes should be landed, nose wheel or not.

Popular modifications to improve performance include several STOL conversion packages, mainly sealing aileron gaps, and a 180-hp engine with constant-speed prop offered by Bush Conversions. As with most Cessna models, you need to make sure the seat rail AD (87-20-3) has been complied with.

Summing up: The 170 is a simple and straightforward machine that is economical to operate and maintain. Its systems remind us of something we once heard Bill Lear say: "You'll never have to replace, repair or maintain anything you leave out."

Table 3-1. Cessna 170 performance & specifications.

Takeoff Distance	700 ft
Takeoff Distance over 50-ft Obstacle	1,500 ft
Landing Distance	500 ft
Landing Distance over 50-ft Obstacle	1,100 ft
Rate of Climb, Maximum Initial	690 ft per min
Service Ceiling	15,500 ft
Maximum Speed	140 mph
Cruise Speed (65% Power)	120 mph
Range at 65% Power	540 mi
Stall, Power Off, No Flaps	58 mph
Stall, Power Off, Flaps Down	52 mph
Engine	Continental C-145
Propeller	McCauley IA170 or Sensenich 73BR-50
Wing Span	36 ft
Length	24 ft 11½ in
Wing Area	175 sq ft
Wing Loading	12.6 lbs per sq ft
Power Loading	15.2 lbs per hp
Height	6 ft 7½ in
Empty Weight	1,205 lbs
Gross Weight	2,200 lbs
Useful Load	995 lbs
Fuel Capacity	42 gal
Baggage Capacity	120 lbs

4

Cessna 180 and 185

WHEN THE CESSNA 180 WAS FIRST INTRODUCED in 1953, it was enthusiastically received by businessmen pilots of that time, and by operators who needed a flying machine in this class with more flexibility than the 170: a nimble load-carrier with a cruise above 150 mph capable of flying from all kinds of fields, including those at high altitudes. Also a good instrument airplane, it was, in short, the flying machine that put the "U" in utility.

The early 180s grossed only 15 percent (350 lbs) more than the 170, but possessed almost 40 percent more horsepower (225-hp vs. 145-hp), and this resulted in a quick-footed craft.

The 180 lost its businessmen buyers, however, when Cessna decided, in 1956, to bring out the 182 (essentially, a 180 with an tricycle landing gear). Nevertheless, the 180 continued in production because a lot of operators in the back-country still found it ideally suited to their requirements and, at the beginning of the seventies, it probably was the most widely used ranch and bush airplane in the world. This is why those of us whose activities take us from one paved runway to another in the "Lower 48," don't see many 180s; they're mostly working in Latin America, Alaska and the American West. More than 5,000 had been built at the end of the sixties.

FEW CHANGES ON 180

The 180 hasn't changed an awful lot over the years. It received five extra horsepower (to 230 hp) in 1956 and its gross weight had grown to 2,800 lbs by 1970, along with increased range (bigger fuel tanks), and an extra window on each side. The 180's nose cowling was redesigned in 1959 for better cooling and additional ram-air pressure to the intake, and the gear legs have been reshaped to obtain a wider track. In 1970, the plane appeared with a few fresh pretties in the cabin. By that time the price—pushed by inflation—was up to $19,725.

In 1973, a new "Camber Lift" wing was added, and only minor changes were made until the last real production year of 1981. In 1992, the going rate for a 1981 model was somewhat over $60,000. This is just about the original retail price for the aircraft—after 10 years of use. Inflation and other factors have certainly driven the price up; in 1953, the first 180 had a list price of $12,950.

1978 C-180 Skywagon

Because the 180 is a working airplane, its cabin is austere with no fancy up-holstery, and its basic interior configuration includes only the pilot's seat. Removable seats for five more passengers are extra-cost items. Flaps are manually operated, and the stabilizer trim wheel and fuel selector switch are located between the seats. It is, in short, an airplane of few surprises—except in the performance department. If you've been flying its citified counterpart (the 182), you'll find that the 180 outperforms the trigear dude in all areas except top speed.

FLIGHT FEELING IN 180

Tailwheel airplanes do require extra skill and experience on the ground and in crosswind landings, and we fail to understand why some av-writers have claimed otherwise. But if you learned to fly in a taildragger, or have some experience in one, you are bound to like the 180. At anything less than full gross load, it'll climb out at 1,000 fpm or better, and its ceiling of almost 20,000 feet promises that it'll take you anywhere and be content with the merest excuse for a landing patch.

The 180 has excellent slow-flight characteristics with a solid control-feel, particularly rudder, and refuses to fully stall with power off and only one or two aboard. It merely shakes a little and bobs its nose seeking a flyable angle-of-attack while determinedly resisting a clean break. She will of course break from power stalls, or even if you are carrying enough weight, power or no power. Even then, this airplane is almost immediately flying again as soon as you relax back-pressure on the wheel.

Among the popular modifications available for the 180 are long-range fuel tanks, an STOL conversion, and wing tip improvements.

Summing up, the 180 is a delightful craft if you prefer to fly the airplane rather than have the airplane fly you.

1974 C-A185F

MORE POWERFUL 185

The Cessna 185 Skywagon is, essentially, a beefed-up 180 with more power. Externally, the airframe might appear to be the same as the 180's, but internally the 185 has additional bracing and a redesigned wing for extra strength. It also has a big dorsal fin that quickly distinguishes it from the 180. The 185 was added to the Cessna utility fleet in 1961. It was fitted with the 260-hp Continental IO-470-F engine through the 185E model of 1966. In that year, Cessna offered the E Model with the IO-520D 300-hp Continental, and in 1967 dropped the 260-hp 180 altogether. The A185E Agcarryall was introduced in 1970, and an agricultural sprayer version was offered in 1972. From 1966 through 1984, Cessna called the 300-hp model the A185E Skywagon.

Skywagon it is. With room for six big people, a useful load of 1,775 lbs (1,620–1,730 lbs for earlier models), and a cruising speed of 169 mph, the 185 sort of picks up where the 180 leaves off—like going from a half-ton to a three-quarter ton pickup, or perhaps more to the point, from a Chevy station wagon to a Buick wagon. It had good performance in 1961, and ten years later (unlike most airplanes) it had not taken on a lot of weight that would subtract from that performance. When the 40 extra horsepower was added, gross weight went up only 150 lbs to 3,350 and empty weight was increased only 15 lbs; therefore, that extra power was available to do some useful work and not wasted on a heavier airframe. To put it another way, the 185, which weighs only 30 lbs more than the 180 (empty), carries 520 lbs more load at about the same speed, 169 vs. 170 mph.

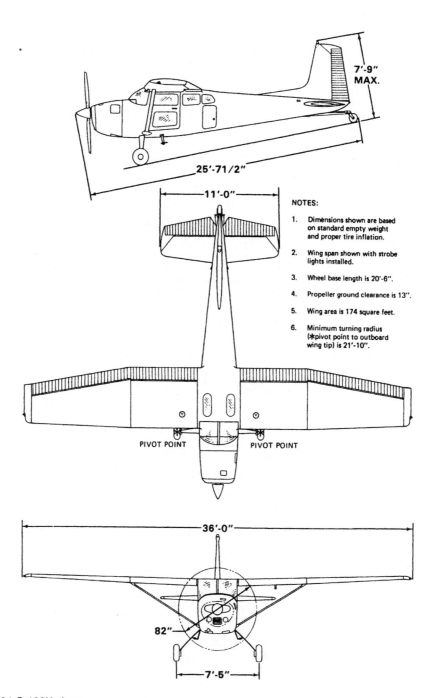

**7'-9"
MAX.**

25'-7 1/2"

11'-0"

NOTES:

1. Dimensions shown are based on standard empty weight and proper tire inflation.

2. Wing span shown with strobe lights installed.

3. Wheel base length is 20'-6".

4. Propeller ground clearance is 13".

5. Wing area is 174 square feet.

6. Minimum turning radius (＊pivot point to outboard wing tip) is 21'-10".

PIVOT POINT   PIVOT POINT

36'-0"

82"

7'-5"

1981 C-180K views

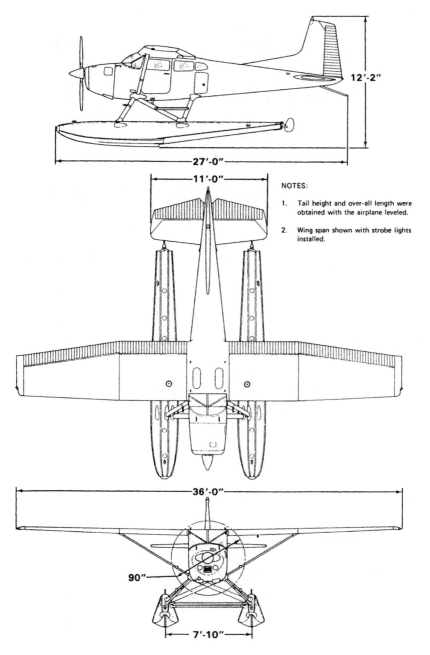

12'-2"

27'-0"

11'-0"

NOTES:

1. Tail height and over-all length were obtained with the airplane leveled.

2. Wing span shown with strobe lights installed.

36'-0"

90"

7'-10"

1981 C-180K floatplane views

IMPROVEMENTS

Between 1971 and 1981, the Cessna 180 accumulated a number of detail and dress-up changes; but the only significant airframe change was the "new wing" introduced with the 1973 model. This airfoil is still a modified NACA 2412, but does provide improved handling, especially in the rolling moment, at low airspeeds. The Skywagon II, with preferred options package, was introduced in 1978.

Dress-up improvements included new fifth and sixth seats that fold flush and need not be removed when converting to cargo configuration, along with a new flap-extension speed (maximum) upped to 140 mph (120 kts). Factory list price for a 1981 model was about $42,000 (price varied with options).

The Cessna 185 Skywagon received a number of detail changes between 1971 and 1984, and an increased maximum allowable flap-extension speed. Most of the changes were for added comfort and convenience.

A few ADs have been issued for the 180. The seat rail AD issued for most Cessna models applies. There have also been some fuel supply problems, most notable is a wrinkled bladder problem requiring special precautions against water accumulation. Quick drains need to be installed, and tanks need to be inspected every 12 months. There is also an AD on wing attachment fittings (73-23-7) and several minor items, such as changes required in the alternator installation.

Table 4-1. 1981 C-180K performance & specifications.

SPEED:

Maximum at Sea Level		148 knots
Cruise, 75% Power at 8000 Ft		142 knots

CRUISE: Recommended lean mixture with fuel allowance for engine start, taxi, takeoff, climb and 45 minutes reserve.

75% Power at 8000 Ft	Range	785 nm
84 Gallons Usable Fuel	Time	5.6 hrs
Maximum Range at 10,000 Ft	Range	1010 nm
84 Gallons Usable Fuel	Time	9.2 hrs

RATE OF CLIMB AT SEA LEVEL	1100 fpm
SERVICE CEILING	17,700 ft

TAKEOFF PERFORMANCE:

Ground Roll	625 ft
Total Distance Over 50-Ft Obstacle	1205 ft

LANDING PERFORMANCE:

Ground Roll	480 ft
Total Distance Over 50-Ft Obstacle	1365 ft

STALL SPEED (KCAS):

Flaps Up, Power Off	53 knots
Flaps Down, Power Off	48 knots

MAXIMUM WEIGHT:

Ramp	2810 lbs
Takeoff or Landing	2800 lbs

STANDARD EMPTY WEIGHT:

180 Skywagon	1650 lbs
180 Skywagon II	1701 lbs

MAXIMUM USEFUL LOAD:

180 Skywagon	1160 lbs
180 Skywagon II	1109 lbs

BAGGAGE ALLOWANCE	170 lbs
WING LOADING: Pounds/Sq Ft	16.1
POWER LOADING: Pounds/HP	12.2
FUEL CAPACITY: Total	88 gal
OIL CAPACITY	12 qts
ENGINE: Teledyne Continental	O-470-U
230 BHP at 2400 RPM	
PROPELLER: Constant Speed, Diameter	82 in

Table 4-2. 1981 C-180K Floatplane performance & specifications.

SPEED:

Maximum at Sea Level	129 knots
Cruise, 75% Power at 8000 Ft	123 knots

CRUISE: Recommended lean mixture with fuel allowance for engine start, taxi, takeoff, climb and 45 minutes reserve.

75% Power at 8000 Ft	Range	680 nm
84 Gallons Usable Fuel	Time	5.6 hrs
Maximum Range at 10,000 Ft	Range	815 nm
84 Gallons Usable Fuel	Time	8.4 hrs

RATE OF CLIMB AT SEA LEVEL — 970 fpm

SERVICE CEILING — 15,300 ft

TAKEOFF PERFORMANCE:

Water Run	1160 ft
Total Distance Over 50-Ft Obstacle	1900 ft

LANDING PERFORMANCE:

Water Run	735 ft
Total Distance Over 50-Ft Obstacle	1720 ft

STALL SPEED (KCAS):

Flaps Up, Power Off	53 knots
Flaps Down, Power Off	48 knots

MAXIMUM WEIGHT:

Ramp (Dock)	2960 lbs
Takeoff or Landing	2950 lbs

STANDARD EMPTY WEIGHT:

180 Skywagon Floatplane	1958 lbs
180 Skywagon II Floatplane	2009 lbs

MAXIMUM USEFUL LOAD:

180 Skywagon Floatplane	1002 lbs
180 Skywagon II Floatplane	951 lbs

BAGGAGE ALLOWANCE — 170 lbs

WING LOADING: Pounds/Sq Ft — 17.0

POWER LOADING: Pounds/HP — 12.8

FUEL CAPACITY: Total — 88 gal

OIL CAPACITY — 12 qts

ENGINE: Teledyne Continental
230 BHP at 2400 RPM — O-470-U

PROPELLER: Constant Speed, Diameter — 90 in

Table 4-3. 1981 C-180K Skiplane performance & specifications.

SPEED:

Maximum at Sea Level	129 knots
Cruise, 75% Power at 8000 Ft	124 knots

CRUISE: Recommended lean mixture with fuel allowance for engine
start, taxi, takeoff, climb and 45 minutes reserve.

75% Power at 8000 Ft	Range	685 nm
84 Gallons Usable Fuel	Time	5.6 hrs
Maximum Range at 10,000 Ft	Range	815 nm
84 Gallons Usable Fuel	Time	8.3 hrs

RATE OF CLIMB AT SEA LEVEL	910 fpm
SERVICE CEILING	14,700 ft

STALL SPEED (KCAS):

Flaps Up, Power Off	53 knots
Flaps Down, Power Off	48 knots

MAXIMUM WEIGHT:

Ramp	2810 lbs
Takeoff or Landing	2800 lbs

STANDARD EMPTY WEIGHT:

180 Skywagon Skiplane	1792 lbs
180 Skywagon II Skiplane	1843 lbs

MAXIMUM USEFUL LOAD:

180 Skywagon Skiplane	1018 lbs
180 Skywagon II Skiplane	967 lbs

BAGGAGE ALLOWANCE	170 lbs
WING LOADING: Pounds/Sq Ft	16.1
POWER LOADING: Pounds/HP	12.2
FUEL CAPACITY: Total	88 gal
OIL CAPACITY	12 qts
ENGINE: Teledyne Continental	O-470-U
230 BHP at 2400 RPM	
PROPELLER: Constant Speed, Diameter	82 in

Table 4-4. 1981 C-180K Amphibian performance & specifications.

SPEED:

Maximum at Sea Level		129 knots
Cruise, 75% Power at 8000 Ft		123 knots

CRUISE: *Recommended lean mixture with fuel allowance for engine start, taxi, takeoff, climb and 45 minutes reserve.*

75% Power at 8000 Ft	Range	680 nm
84 Gallons Usable Fuel	Time	5.6 hrs
Maximum Range at 10,000 Ft	Range	815 nm
84 Gallons Usable Fuel	Time	8.4 hrs

RATE OF CLIMB AT SEA LEVEL 970 fpm

SERVICE CEILING 15,300 ft

	ON LAND	ON WATER
TAKEOFF PERFORMANCE:		
Ground Roll (or Water Run)	700 ft	1160 ft
Total Distance Over 50-Ft Obstacle	1315 ft	1900 ft
LANDING PERFORMANCE:		
Ground Roll (or Water Run)	740 ft	735 ft
Total Distance Over 50-Ft Obstacle	1450 ft	1720 ft
STALL SPEED (KCAS):		
Flaps Up, Power Off		53 knots
Flaps Down, Power Off		48 knots
MAXIMUM WEIGHT:		
Ramp (Dock)		2960 lbs
Takeoff or Landing		2950 lbs
STANDARD EMPTY WEIGHT:		
180 Skywagon Amphibian		2213 lbs
180 Skywagon II Amphibian		2264 lbs
MAXIMUM USEFUL LOAD:		
180 Skywagon Amphibian		747 lbs
180 Skywagon II Amphibian		696 lbs

BAGGAGE ALLOWANCE 170 lbs

WING LOADING: *Pounds/Sq Ft* 17.0

POWER LOADING: *Pounds/HP* 12.8

FUEL CAPACITY: *Total* 88 gal

OIL CAPACITY 12 qts

ENGINE: *Teledyne Continental* O-470-U
230 BHP at 2400 RPM

PROPELLER: *Constant Speed, Diameter* 90 in

Table 4-5. 1985 Skywagon (A185F) performance & specifications.

SPEED:

Maximum at Sea Level	154 knots
Cruise, 75% Power at 7000 Ft	147 knots

CRUISE: Recommended lean mixture with fuel allowance for engine start, taxi, takeoff, climb and 45 minutes reserve.

75% Power at 7000 Ft	Range	645 nm
84 Gallons Usable Fuel	Time	4.5 hrs
Maximum Range at 10,000 Ft	Range	850 nm
84 Gallons Usable Fuel	Time	7.4 hrs

RATE OF CLIMB AT SEA LEVEL	1075 fpm
SERVICE CEILING	17,900 ft

TAKEOFF PERFORMANCE:

Ground Roll	825 ft
Total Distance Over 50-Ft Obstacle	1430 ft

LANDING PERFORMANCE:

Ground Roll	610 ft
Total Distance Over 50-Ft Obstacle	1400 ft

STALL SPEED (KCAS):

Flaps Up, Power Off	56 knots
Flaps Down, Power Off	49 knots

MAXIMUM WEIGHT:

Ramp	3362 lbs
Takeoff or Landing	3350 lbs

STANDARD EMPTY WEIGHT:

185 Skywagon	1726 lbs

MAXIMUM USEFUL LOAD:

185 Skywagon	1636 lbs

BAGGAGE ALLOWANCE	170 lbs
WING LOADING: Pounds/Sq Ft	19.3
POWER LOADING: Pounds/HP	11.2
FUEL CAPACITY: Total	88 gal
OIL CAPACITY	13 qts

ENGINE: Teledyne Continental, Fuel Injection   IO-520-D
         300 BHP at 2850 RPM (5-Minute Takeoff Rating)
         285 BHP at 2700 RPM (Maximum Continuous Rating)

PROPELLER: 3-Bladed Constant Speed, Diameter   80 in

5

Cessna 172, 175, 172RG

THE 172 AND SKYHAWK OWNER, who represents at least 10 percent of general aviation, has largely been misunderstood by the old hands in this business whose lives have always revolved around airplanes. Those of us who never wanted to be anything but a "pilot" from the time we were nine years old (that seemed to us a lofty ambition indeed), have been puzzled by all these bright young men ("newcomers") who buy and fly modern lightplanes merely for the sake of convenience.

It's the Generation Gap, Dad. The Travel Air 4000 and the grass landing patches we remember with such fondness possess no more relevance for today's young man on the way up than did the horse and buggy for us. The average Skyhawk owner probably never heard of a Gee Bee Racer; and what's more, he hasn't time to listen while we tell him about it with a faraway look in our eye. The horrible truth is, he's not interested.

Cessna recognized the emergence of this new breed and correctly assessed its attitude back in the mid-fifties. Clearly, there was a big and growing market for a four-place business/pleasure aircraft that did not demand professional-type skills and experience for its safe operation. A practical machine to serve the man who regarded a personal airplane as a kind of supercar is the Cessna 172/Skyhawk.

The 172 was introduced in 1956, and it was, in effect, a 170 with tricycle landing gear and 180 tail. This happy combination was squarely on target; and though it has submitted to a number of changes over the year—mostly to make it prettier— the 1971 Model 172 and Skyhawk was still pretty close to the original, performance-wise, as a look at the model comparison charts (following chapter 10) reveals.

FLIGHT EVALUATIONS

A brief flight evaluation of a 1957 Model 172, followed by checks of a 1962 Skyhawk, 1968 Skyhawk and 1986 Skyhawk, should provide good representative coverage of this series. The Skyhawk, as you undoubtedly know, is simply the deluxe version of the 172, the principal differences being that the Skyhawk has a full gyro panel activated by an internal vacuum system, full paint job, and speed fairings on the wheels.

1986 Skyhawk

The 1957 Model 172 was in excellent condition and as neat inside as TLC (tender loving care) could keep it after thirteen years. Our only beef was that the flight instruments were not well grouped, but had apparently been stuck in the panel at random. An aging mechanic insisted that this was Cessna's standard arrangement for that airplane. Maybe so, we couldn't remember.

This craft sits a little higher off the ground than later models, and the old starter pull-knob is right beside the parking brake, making it easy to grab the wrong one. Otherwise, you feel right at home in this plane if you've flown later Cessnas. Firing up the engine and taxiing is standard Cessna; it rolls easily with the merest hint of power. The nosewheel's steerability is fairly limited via the rudder pedals, but it will swivel through an arc of about 30 degrees by applying full rudder and toe-brake for tight turns on the ground.

Takeoff was the same now-famous "drive'er down the runway and into the air" of later Cessnas. Then, with three aboard and full tanks (about 230 lbs below gross of 2,200 lbs), the '57 Model showed an initial climb of 500 fpm at 78 mph on a warmish day. At 6,500 ft with 2,400 rpms, which we judged to be 65 percent power, the IAS (indicated air speed) was 106 mph. Corrected for temperature and altitude, this worked out to slightly over 120 mph TAS (true air speed). This latter figure was determined courtesy of Mr. Dalton's E-6B Computer; but we must confess to an attachment for the ancient (a la Travel Air days) method of arriving at this number by simply adding 2 percent per thousand feet of altitude to the IAS. It's not precise, but usually close enough for lightplane VFR when lapse rates are normal.

STANDARD STALLS

Stall characteristics of Cessna's 1957 Model supercar are also standard Cessna, which is to say you have to work at it to force this airplane into full-stall with

1958 C-175

power off. It prefers to just sit there and mush along with the stall warning horn assaulting your ears and the airspeed indicator bumping at 50 mph. It's easier to make the plane break from a stall with power on, but the airspeed falls clear down to 40 mph on the dial. Some aileron control remains even at these indicated speeds, but it's probably wiser to level the wings with the rudder, especially if the flaps are down, and even more especially if you're at or near gross load. We're not sure whether it would happen with a Cessna, but we do know that sudden aileron movement in or near the stall will add just enough drag on the down-aileron side to stall-out that wing and induce a quick spin on some airplanes.

The owner of this airplane demonstrated landings holding a final approach speed of 70 mph. He touched-down on the main wheels in a full-stall from the flare, and allowed the nosewheel to come down immediately. This is the "drive it back on the ground" method and seems to work very well for a lot of people, although many instructors used to recommend holding the nosewheel off until it eased down of its own accord. With the nosewheel on the pavement, one does have much easier and better control, however. Also, the Cessna nosewheel is attached to the airframe rather than the engine mount, and for short-field landings, the Owner's Manual advises that the nosewheel be put down immediately after touchdown.

1962 SKYHAWK

The 1962 Skyhawk we checked was also well-equipped and in top condition. Except for its paint scheme, differently shaped speed fairings on the wheels, and lack of a rear window, it closely resembled its newer sisters. Inside, the instrument panel held the six flight instruments in two rows directly in front of the pilot (airspeed, directional gyro and attitude gyro across the top; altimeter, turn/bank and rate-of-climb

1977 Hawk XP

across the bottom). Engine controls were grouped at bottom-center of panel, of course, along with the fuel-sump drain knob. It's a matter of opinion, but in our view there are a few things necessary to a happy flight that should be checked visually and positively, like fuel tanks, oil level, tires, and the like, and we just don't trust that painless (and blind) sump-drain operation from inside the cabin.

Fuel is gravity-fed to the 145-hp Continental O-300-D engine via the fuel selector switch located between the front seats. Its positions are Off, Left, Right and Both, although we get the impression that few pilots ever use fuel from the left or right tank individually. Total fuel is 42 gallons, with slightly less than 41 usable.

Engine starting procedure is standard: Battery switch, "ON," mixture set at "Full Rich," throttle slightly cracked, a couple of squirts of primer and turn ignition key past "Both" to start. We note that this owner checks his mags at 1,700 rpms, pivots his Skyhawk in a complete 360-degree circle so he can get a look at the entire pattern around this uncontrolled field, then drives down the runway and into the air, lifting off at about 60 mph without flaps. It is a cool day, about 50 degrees Fat field elevation of 1,180 ft. The takeoff run is estimated at 750 feet, with two of us aboard and full tanks (340 lbs below gross).

Initial climb registers 900+ fpm with maximum power and 70 mph. This drops back to 500 fpm as we lower the nose and increase speed to 100 mph with 2,500 rpms. Our host tells us that the 1962 Skyhawk's best cruising speed comes at 7,000 feet, where 2,500 rpms produces about 134 mph TAS for him. However, we stayed at 3,500 where 116 mph IAS translated into 124 mph TAS at 38 degrees F. Our friend told us that his 2,500 rpm cruise consumed 8½ gallons of fuel per hour.

Returning to his home field, our host drove his Skyhawk onto the runway holding 70 mph over the fence and let his nosewheel come down almost immediately after the main wheels touched. He then raised his flaps and held a little backpressure on the control wheel during rollout. He braked sparingly into a 3–5 mph wind and used an estimated 600 feet of runway.

1985 Cutlass RG

1968 SKYHAWK

The 1968 Skyhawk had recently had a thorough workout at the hands of our colleague, Miss Page Shamburger. Page has about 5,000 hours in her logbook and now owns a Bonanza; but she started out in Cessnas (140s and 170s), and says she "feels right at home with these fellers." Because she spent considerable time in a Skyhawk, we asked her for her impressions.

"Beginning with this 1968 Model, the 172/Skyhawk has the 150-hp 'Blue Streak' Lycoming engine," Page said, "but I really can't see where it adds anything, except maybe a little dab of useful load. This is because the 1968 Model is 40 pounds lighter than the '67 Model. Gross remains at 2,300 pounds, where it has been since 1963.

"Inside, instruments are T-grouped, and dry vacuum pumps have replaced the plumbing and oil-lubricated pumps for gyro instruments. Electrically operated flaps are standard on both the 172 and Skyhawk. The rear-vision mirror, by the way, costs $20 extra, and I found it useless, at least for rear-visioning.

"Normal engine-start procedures awaken the Lycoming's hundred-and-fifty horses, and I thought this airplane seemed markedly quieter inside, probably because the twin exhaust stacks of the Continental-powered Skyhawks and 172s have been changed to a single and longer stack on the Lycoming-engined craft.

"(Because) this airplane was a factory demonstrator, it was loaded with avionics and extras, bringing its empty weight up to 1,407 pounds. However, I had left 893 pounds useful, which seemed enough for most anything. Checking my notes, I'm reminded that, taxiing out, the shorter nose strut, introduced in 1967 to reduce in-flight drag, also allows you to see the concrete very close ahead.

"With 297 pounds of people (two hundred for Cessna's John Gallaher; ninety-seven for me), and full tanks, I was 340 pounds under gross. And according to my notes, I lifted-off in less than 800 feet at 65 mph (elevation, 1,370 ft), and remarked on the secure feeling of the Skyhawk even during those early, crucial seconds of flight. I felt that I had stability to spare. I climbed at 85 mph showing 750 fpm.

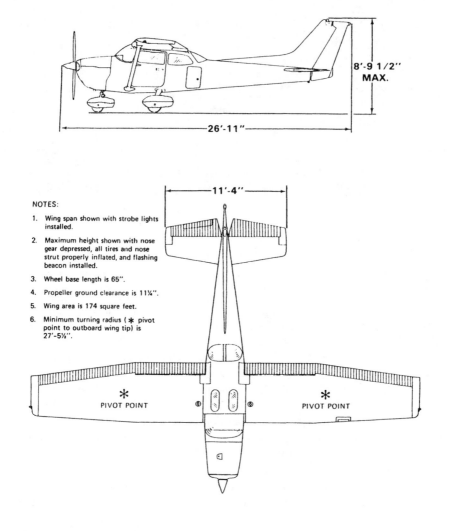

NOTES:

1. Wing span shown with strobe lights installed.

2. Maximum height shown with nose gear depressed, all tires and nose strut properly inflated, and flashing beacon installed.

3. Wheel base length is 65".

4. Propeller ground clearance is 11¼".

5. Wing area is 174 square feet.

6. Minimum turning radius (✳ pivot point to outboard wing tip) is 27'-5½".

8'-9 1/2" MAX.

26'-11"

11'-4"

✳ PIVOT POINT   ✳ PIVOT POINT

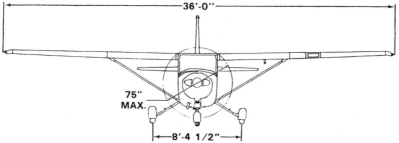

36'-0"

75" MAX.

8'-4 1/2"

1986 Skyhawk (172P) views

]

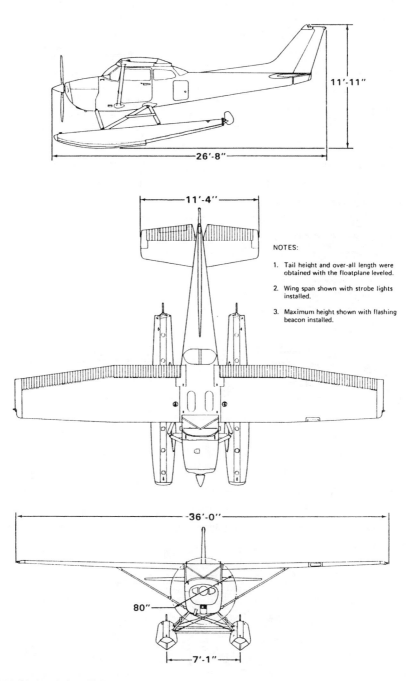

11'-11"

26'-8"

11'-4"

NOTES:

1. Tail height and over-all length were obtained with the floatplane leveled.

2. Wing span shown with strobe lights installed.

3. Maximum height shown with flashing beacon installed.

36'-0"

80"

7'-1"

1986 Skyhawk (172P) floatplane views

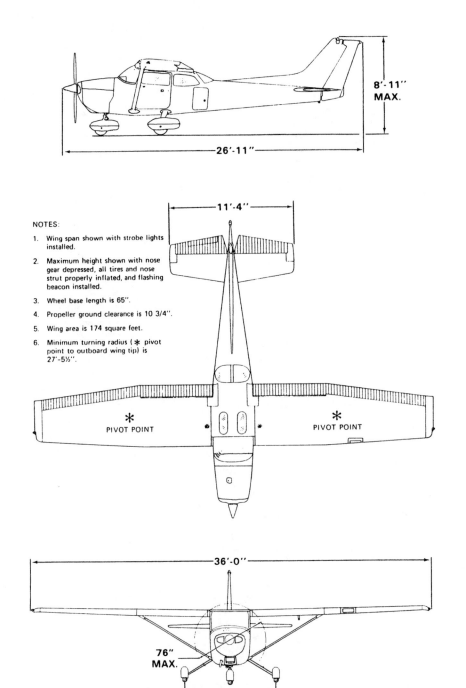

NOTES:

1. Wing span shown with strobe lights installed.

2. Maximum height shown with nose gear depressed, all tires and nose strut properly inflated, and flashing beacon installed.

3. Wheel base length is 65".

4. Propeller ground clearance is 10 3/4".

5. Wing area is 174 square feet.

6. Minimum turning radius (✳ pivot point to outboard wing tip) is 27'-5½".

✳ PIVOT POINT ✳ PIVOT POINT

1983 Cutlass (172Q) views

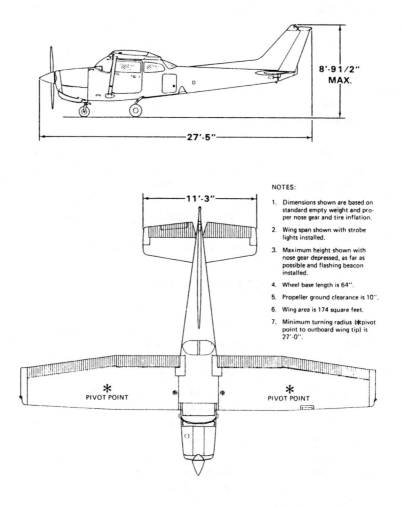

NOTES:

1. Dimensions shown are based on standard empty weight and proper nose gear and tire inflation.

2. Wing span shown with strobe lights installed.

3. Maximum height shown with nose gear depressed, as far as possible and flashing beacon installed.

4. Wheel base length is 64".

5. Propeller ground clearance is 10".

6. Wing area is 174 square feet.

7. Minimum turning radius (✴pivot point to outboard wing tip) is 27'-0".

8'-9 1/2" MAX.

27'-5"

11'-3"

✴ PIVOT POINT

✴ PIVOT POINT

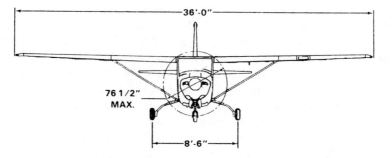

36'-0"

76 1/2" MAX.

8'-6"

1985 Cutlass RG (172RG) views

"Leveling off at 10,500 feet, I found my TAS by using the handy computer on the airspeed indicator. This is a rotating bezel mounted on the periphery of that instrument. You rotate it to set pressure altitude opposite outside air temperature (OAT), then read true air speed directly below the indicator needle. With an OAT of 22 degrees, I had 134 mph true at 65 percent power.

"During let-down for Oklahoma City, I tried some stalls and was intrigued with the prestall warning given by the reeds inside the wing that cry at an increasingly-higher pitch as the wing gets nearer the stall. This simple system works from air pressure flowing over the reeds, and no exterior sensor vane—so vulnerable to accidental bending—is needed. Straight ahead, with flaps up and power off, the nose sticks way up in the air, where the controls get heavy enough to prompt you to crank in some elevator trim (via the control located on the center console). Then this airplane broke clean at 50 mph indicated—57 mph corrected— shaking and whistling frantically at me for mistreating it so. Flaps lower the stall to 41 IAS (49 mph corrected), and the nose-up angle is strictly unreal.

"Landings? Well, it's a Cessna, just no problem. I did the first one holding 80 mph, and flaring at that speed produced some ballooning. Second time around, with half-flaps and indicating 73 mph, I put it where I wanted it and it stayed there."

1971 SKYHAWK

The 1971 Skyhawk/172 possessed a few improvements over previous models, the main one being a switch to the Cardinal-proved tubular landing gear legs. These tapered tubular struts, encased in streamlined housings, are superior to the "slab steel" struts because they absorb shocks fore and aft, as well as up and down. In our view, this is the most practical, versatile and trouble free landing gear offered on any light airplane. We first encountered this gear back in November, 1967, when it was introduced on the original Cardinal/177. We were sold on it then. We still are. If you think the Skyhawk/172 has been easy to land in the past, this gear is, surely, the meringue on that piece of pie.

The 1971 Model also had restyled wheel fairings. Cessna apparently reshapes these things more for model identification than anything else. The latest ones might look racy, but they are undoubtedly less efficient aerodynamically than the old fashioned teardrop shape.

Other new features for 1971 included a redesigned nose cap to eliminate propeller "slap" noise in the cabin and nose-mounted landing light. Optional were new overhead windows, wingtip strobe lights (white), a hands-off boom microphone and full paint job on the 172 version. The fully-articulating seats, introduced on the 1970 Model, may be adjusted to any position from fully reclined to full forward, and through a wide range of heights. The '71 Model, for the first time, offered "gen-u-wine" leather upholstery as an option with the Skyhawk. Most impressive of all, perhaps, was the welcome news in 1971 that the 150-hp Lycoming engine had a recommended time between overhaul of 2,000 hours. When Cessna switched to this engine in 1968, recommended TBO was 1,500 hours. It was 1,200 hours for the O-300 Continental in earlier Skyhawk/172s.

For total utility, the redesigned instrument panel of the 1971 Model offers plenty of space for magical black boxes, including 300 Nav-O-Matic autopilot, 300 Transceiver, 90- and 360-channel Nav/Coms, ADF, Marker Beacon, Glideslope Receiver, the 300 Transponder with a reply code capability of up to 4,096 with Modes A and AC, and the ARC (Cessna) DME.

List price of the basic 172 for 1971 was $13,425, and the '71 Skyhawk list was $14,995. Reflecting the enormous pricing increases over the intervening years, the last Skyhawks produced in 1986 listed at $74,000 with average equipment. In 1992, a 1986 Skyhawk went for about $70,000, losing little, if any, value.

CONVERSIONS AND ADS

As the best selling of Cessna's lightplanes, the 172 has also proved popular with the conversion people. Among the popular modifications for the 172 are taildragger conversion, replacing the tricycle gear with conventional; long-range tanks; various STOL kits; a 180-hp engine with constant-speed prop conversion; wingtip replacements; and baggage compartment fuel tanks. One modification package offered a Porsche engine installation.

Numerous ADs apply to various models, few of the ADs apply to all 172s. First, there is the common seat-rail AD; several ADs against the Lycoming O-360 and O-320 engines, generally involving the valves; one on the nosegear fork; and several control items, such as elevator control (81-16-9). You should check carefully for outstanding ADs against the model you are interested in.

The Army and Air Force Cessna T-41 is the military version of the 172. It was adopted as the primary Air Force trainer in 1965. The T-41A was a basic 172 model; the T41B, delivered in 1967 (called the Mescalero), the T41C (1968) and the T41D (1968) were 210 hp versions based upon a Reims Rocket version.

Cessna introduced a number of souped-up versions of the 172 through the years. Whenever more horsepower was needed at the low end of the market, the 172 was the logical base. None of these models lasted long on the market, but some sold in significant quantity during their lifespan. The most important of these models are the 175/Skylark, the Hawk XP, and the Cutlass/Cutlass RG.

175

The Cessna 175/Skylark was brought out in 1958 and, for a couple of years, sold almost as well as the 172/Skyhawk (the Skyhawk version of the 172 first appeared in 1959), but the 175 slipped badly in sales in 1961, and production ended in 1963, at which time Cessna briefly called this airplane the "172 Powermatic."

The 175/Skylark and Powermatic is basically a 172 airframe fitted with the Continental GO-300-E engine of 175 hp, and constant-speed propeller. The GO-300-E is a geared mill that produces its maximum power at 2,400 propeller rpms while the crankshaft rpms register 3,200, a ratio of 0.75:1. Because the propeller reduction-gear box is located above the drive shaft on the front of the engine, the same 84-inch propeller as used on the 145-hp engines gains a couple of inches in ground clearance. And because this is the same engine as the 145-hp O-300-D employed by Skyhawks of this period—except for the gearing—it's obvious that the additional 30 horsepower results from the higher crankshaft speed, and that clearly can't add anything to engine life or reliability.

This model has an extra knob in the cockpit: the prop pitch control. It is also a push-pull type and changes the setting of the propeller governor to control engine speed. This control may be moved through its full range by depressing a locking button in the center of the knob, while minor adjustments are made by releasing the locking button and rotating the knob—clockwise to increase rpms and counterclockwise to decrease rpms.

For all ground operations and takeoff, the propeller control should be full in (high rpms). After takeoff, reduce throttle first, then reduce rpms. Because a small control movement will produce a considerable rpm change, you should set up climb and cruise rpms by screwing the knob in or out.

This airplane also has cowl flaps that are not found on comparable models of the 172. These of course merely control the flow of air over the engine for greater efficiency under varying conditions. Opening the cowl flaps on the ground and during steep climbs, for example, improves engine cooling. In flight, closing the flaps reduces the cooling air to the engine and reduces drag. This control is a double-button type with a friction lock.

These planes use the same fuel system as that of the 172/Skyhawk, except that capacity is 10 gallons greater. Most modifications available for the 172 are also available for the 175.

This series of course has improved performance compared to the standard 172s, but the difference was probably not great enough to warrant the extra cost. The 1958 Cessna 175 had a basic list of $10,995 vs. $8,995 for the 172. By 1963, the "Powermatic 172" was priced at $13,275 vs. $10,245 for the 172, while the 1963 "Skyhawk Powermatic" sold for $14,650 vs. $11,995 for the 1963 145-hp Skyhawk.

HAWK XP

The Hawk XP (eXtra Performance) series was introduced in 1977, with a 195-hp Continental IO-360 engine and a constant-speed prop. This version lasted until 1981. It was popular as a floatplane, where the extra horsepower came in particularly handy. The Hawk XP was based upon a 210-hp modified 172 introduced by Reims Aviation, in France, as the Reims Rocket, and is also close in design to the military T-41D (the T-41D has a 210 hp engine).

A 1980 Hawk XP II (preferred options package) had a base retail price of $39,450; the 1992 used price for this craft is about $40,000.

One popular Hawk XP conversion is a taildragger refit. The extra power makes a taildragger Hawk XP an excellent bush plane.

172RG

Another significant variant of the 172 design is the Cutlass, introduced in 1980 as a retractable-gear 172, with the model designation C-172RG. In 1983, a fixed gear version, the C-172Q, was introduced. While the Cutlass fixed-gear model lasted two years, the Cutlass RG continued up to 1985.

The Cutlass RG has a gross weight of 2,650 lbs., and is powered by a 180-hp Lycoming (O-360-FIA6) engine. It features a constant-speed prop, electro-hydraulic landing gear mechanism, preselect flap control, reclining seats and other features. The fixed-gear version was powered by the same engine and weighed in at slightly less. The Cutlass RG is known for its range and endurance, and would probably have been a star in the Cessna lineup if the market hadn't collapsed just when it was introduced.

The 1985 Cutlass RG had a base price of $76,850; in 1992, the same plane would bring about the same price (or more) on the used market—with standard equipment. A 1984 Cutlass (172Q II) went for $61,400 base retail, and that plane would bring about $50,000 on the 1992 used market with standard equipment.

Table 5-1. Skylark (175) and Powermatic performance & specifications.

	175 (1958)	Powermatic (1963)
Engine	Continental	Continental
Wingspan	G0-300-E	G0-300-E
Length	36 ft 2 in	36 ft 2 in
Height	25 ft	26 ft 6 in
Wing Area	8 ft 6 in	8 ft 11 in
Gross Weight	174 sq ft	174 sq ft
Wing Loading	2,350 lbs	2,500 lbs
Power Loading	13.5 lbs sq ft	14.4 lbs/hp
Useful Load	945 lbs	1,140 lbs
Fuel Capacity	52 gals	52 gals
Takeoff	640 ft	600 ft
clear 50 ft	1,340 ft	1,205 ft
Landing	600 ft	610 ft
clear 50 ft	1,155 ft	1200 ft
Climb (Initial)	850 fpm	830 fpm
Service Ceiling	17,800 ft	17,000 ft
Maximum Speed	147 mph	146 mph
Cruise (75%)	140 mph	138 mph
Range (@75%)	585 mi	540 mi
Stall (no flaps)	58 mph	64 mph
Stall		
(flaps 40-deg)	50 mph	55 mph

Table 5-2. 1986 Skyhawk (172P) performance & specifications.

SPEED:

Maximum at Sea Level		123 knots
Cruise, 75% Power at 8000 Ft		120 knots

CRUISE: *Recommended lean mixture with fuel allowance for engine start, taxi, takeoff, climb and 45 minutes reserve.*

75% Power at 8000 Ft	Range	440 nm
40 Gallons Usable Fuel	Time	3.8 hrs
75% Power at 8000 Ft	Range	585 nm
50 Gallons Usable Fuel	Time	5.0 hrs
75% Power at 8000 Ft	Range	755 nm
62 Gallons Usable Fuel	Time	6.4 hrs
Maximum Range at 10,000 Ft	Range	520 nm
40 Gallons Usable Fuel	Time	5.6 hrs
Maximum Range at 10,000 Ft	Range	680 nm
50 Gallons Usable Fuel	Time	7.4 hrs
Maximum Range at 10,000 Ft	Range	875 nm
62 Gallons Usable Fuel	Time	9.4 hrs

RATE OF CLIMB AT SEA LEVEL — 700 fpm

SERVICE CEILING — 13,000 ft

TAKEOFF PERFORMANCE:

Ground Roll	890 ft
Total Distance Over 50-Ft Obstacle	1625 ft

LANDING PERFORMANCE:

Ground Roll	540 ft
Total Distance Over 50-Ft Obstacle	1280 ft

STALL SPEED (KCAS):

Flaps Up, Power Off	51 knots
Flaps Down, Power Off	46 knots

MAXIMUM WEIGHT:

Ramp	2407 lbs
Takeoff or Landing	2400 lbs

STANDARD EMPTY WEIGHT — 1433 lbs

MAXIMUM USEFUL LOAD — 974 lbs

BAGGAGE ALLOWANCE — 120 lbs

WING LOADING: *Pounds/Sq Ft* — 13.8

POWER LOADING: *Pounds/HP* — 15.0

FUEL CAPACITY: *Total*

Standard Tanks	43 gal
Long Range Tanks	54 gal
Integral Tanks	68 gal

OIL CAPACITY — 8 qts

ENGINE: *Avco Lycoming*   O-320-D2J
160 BHP at 2700 RPM

PROPELLER: *Fixed Pitch, Diameter* — 75 in

Table 5-3. 1986 Skyhawk (172P) Floatplane performance & specifications.

SPEED:

Maximum at Sea Level		96 knots
Cruise, 75% Power at 4000 Ft		95 knots

CRUISE: Recommended lean mixture with fuel allowance for engine start, taxi, takeoff, climb and 45 minutes reserve.

75% Power at 4000 Ft	Range		360 nm
40 Gallons Usable Fuel		Time	3.8 hrs
75% Power at 4000 Ft		Range	475 nm
50 Gallons Usable Fuel		Time	5.0 hrs
Maximum Range at 10,000 Ft		Range	435 nm
40 Gallons Usable Fuel		Time	5.6 hrs
Maximum Range at 10,000 Ft		Range	565 nm
50 Gallons Usable Fuel		Time	7.3 hrs

RATE OF CLIMB AT SEA LEVEL	740 fpm
SERVICE CEILING	15,000 ft

TAKEOFF PERFORMANCE:

Water Run	1400 ft
Total Distance Over 50-Ft Obstacle	2160 ft

LANDING PERFORMANCE:

Water Run	590 ft
Total Distance Over 50-Ft Obstacle	1345 ft

STALL SPEED (KCAS):

Flaps Up, Power Off	48 knots
Flaps Down, Power Off	44 knots

MAXIMUM WEIGHT:

Ramp (Dock)	2227 lbs
Takeoff or Landing	2220 lbs

STANDARD EMPTY WEIGHT	1615 lbs
MAXIMUM USEFUL LOAD	612 lbs
BAGGAGE ALLOWANCE	120 lbs
WING LOADING: Pounds/Sq Ft	12.7
POWER LOADING: Pounds/HP	13.9

FUEL CAPACITY: Total

Standard Tanks	43 gal
Long Range Tanks	54 gal

OIL CAPACITY	8 qts
ENGINE: Avco Lycoming	O-320-D2J
160 BHP at 2700 RPM	
PROPELLER: Fixed Pitch, Diameter	80 in

Table 5-4. 1978 Hawk XP performance & specifications.

SPEED:

Maximum at Sea Level	133 knots	246 kph
Cruise, 80% Power at 6000 Ft	130 knots	241 kph

CRUISE: Recommended lean mixture with fuel
allowance for engine start, taxi, takeoff,
climb and 45 minutes reserve at 45% power

80% Power at 6000 Ft with	480 nm	889 km
49 Gallons Usable Fuel	3.7 hr	3.7 hr
Maximum Range at 10,000 Ft	575 nm	1065 km
with 49 Gallons Usable Fuel	6.1 hr	6.1 hr

RATE OF CLIMB AT SEA LEVEL	870 fpm	265 mpm
SERVICE CEILING	17,000 ft	5182 m

TAKEOFF PERFORMANCE:

Ground Roll	800 ft	244 m
Total Distance Over 50-Ft Obstacle	1360 ft	415 m

LANDING PERFORMANCE:

Ground Roll	620 ft	189 m
Total Distance Over 50-Ft Obstacle	1270 ft	387 m

STALL SPEED, (CAS):

Flaps Up, Power Off	53 knots	98 kph
Flaps Down, Power Off	46 knots	85 kph

MAXIMUM WEIGHT	2550 lb	1157 kg

STANDARD EMPTY WEIGHT:

Hawk XP	1531 lb	695 kg
Hawk XP II	1557 lb	706 kg

MAXIMUM USEFUL LOAD:

Hawk XP	1019 lb	462 kg
Hawk XP II	993 lb	451 kg

BAGGAGE ALLOWANCE	200 lb	91 kg
WING LOADING	14.7 lb/sq ft	71.6 kg/sq m
POWER LOADING	13.1 lb/hp	5.9 kg/hp
WING SPAN	35 ft, 10 in	10.92 m
WING AREA	174 sq ft	16.16 sq m
LENGTH	27 ft, 2 in	8.28 m
HEIGHT	8 ft, 9½ in	2.68 m
FUEL CAPACITY: Total	52 gal	197 liters
OIL CAPACITY	8 qt	7.6 liters

ENGINE: Teledyne-Continental IO-360-K Fuel
Injection Engine; 195 BHP at 2600 RPM

PROPELLER: Constant Speed,
76 In Diameter (1.93 m)

Table 5-5. 1983 Cutlass performance & specifications.

SPEED:

Maximum at Sea Level		124 knots
Cruise, 75% Power at 8500 Ft		122 knots

CRUISE: Recommended lean mixture with fuel allowance for engine start, taxi, takeoff, climb and 45 minutes reserve.

75% Power at 8500 Ft	Range	475 nm
50 Gallons Usable Fuel	Time	4.0 hrs
75% Power at 8500 Ft	Range	620 nm
62 Gallons Usable Fuel	Time	5.2 hrs
Maximum Range at 10,000 Ft	Range	600 nm
50 Gallons Usable Fuel	Time	6.4 hrs
Maximum Range at 10,000 Ft	Range	775 nm
62 Gallons Usable Fuel	Time	8.2 hrs

RATE OF CLIMB AT SEA LEVEL — 680 fpm

SERVICE CEILING — 17,000 ft

TAKEOFF PERFORMANCE:

Ground Roll	960 ft
Total Distance Over 50-Ft Obstacle	1690 ft

LANDING PERFORMANCE:

Ground Roll	575 ft
Total Distance Over 50-Ft Obstacle	1335 ft

STALL SPEED (KCAS):

Flaps Up, Power Off	53 knots
Flaps Down, Power Off	48 knots

MAXIMUM WEIGHT:

Ramp	2558 lbs
Takeoff or Landing	2550 lbs

STANDARD EMPTY WEIGHT:

Cutlass	1486 lbs
Cutlass II	1513 lbs

MAXIMUM USEFUL LOAD:

Cutlass	1072 lbs
Cutlass II	1045 lbs

BAGGAGE ALLOWANCE — 120 lbs

WING LOADING: Pounds/Sq Ft — 14.7

POWER LOADING: Pounds/HP — 14.2

FUEL CAPACITY: Total

Standard Tanks	54 gal
Long Range Tanks	68 gal

OIL CAPACITY — 9 qts

ENGINE: Avco Lycoming
180 BHP at 2700 RPM — O-360-A4N

PROPELLER: Fixed Pitch, Diameter — 76 in

Table 5-6. 1985 Cutlass RG performance & specifications.

SPEED:

Maximum at Sea Level	145 knots
Cruise, 75% Power at 9000 Ft	140 knots

CRUISE: Recommended lean mixture with fuel allowance for engine start, taxi, takeoff, climb and 45 minutes reserve.

75% Power at 9000 Ft	Range	720 nm
62 Gallons Usable Fuel	Time	5.3 hrs
Maximum Range at 10,000 Ft	Range	840 nm
62 Gallons Usable Fuel	Time	7.7 hrs

RATE OF CLIMB AT SEA LEVEL	800 fpm
SERVICE CEILING	16,800 ft

TAKEOFF PERFORMANCE:

Ground Roll	1060 ft
Total Distance Over 50-Ft Obstacle	1775 ft

LANDING PERFORMANCE:

Ground Roll	625 ft
Total Distance Over 50-Ft Obstacle	1340 ft

STALL SPEED (KCAS):

Flaps Up, Power Off	54 knots
Flaps Down, Power Off	50 knots

MAXIMUM WEIGHT:

Ramp	2658 lbs
Takeoff or Landing	2650 lbs

STANDARD EMPTY WEIGHT	1600 lbs
MAXIMUM USEFUL LOAD	1058 lbs
BAGGAGE ALLOWANCE	200 lbs
WING LOADING: Pounds/Sq Ft	15.2
POWER LOADING: Pounds/HP	14.7
FUEL CAPACITY: Total	66 gal
OIL CAPACITY	9 qts
ENGINE: Avco Lycoming 180 BHP at 2700 RPM	O-360-F1A6
PROPELLER: Constant Speed, Diameter	76.5 in

6

Cessna 177

WHEN THE FIRST 177 and Cardinal was introduced in November, 1967, with a swinging party for dealers and av-writers at Cessna's Wichita Delivery Center, we were there for a serious look at this all-new design. While most of our colleagues were swapping lies, enjoying the Dixieland band and stuffing themselves with bar-b-que, we slipped off with a company checkpilot for an afternoon of air work in 2207Y, one of the first Cardinals built (1968 Model).

We liked that airplane, and found almost nothing to pick at. However, owners soon discovered to their horror that it didn't fly or land exactly like a strutless Sky-hawk, and some heavy-handed supercar drivers managed to smash the Cardinal tail into the pavement on landing, knock-off a few nose-wheels, etc. (Apparently, this was possible if one closed his eyes, used full back-pressure on the wheel at the flare and then sat rigidly waiting for the crashing noises to subside).

Cessna accepted the blame gracefully. That was proper because, after all, they had lulled a generation of Cessna pilots into near-effortless flying with the extremely forgiving 172 series, and it probably wasn't ethical to suddenly offer, to many of those same customers, a Cessna that didn't handle exactly like a Cessna. The company therefore picked up the tab for a list of modifications that gentled the Cardinal and returned the smiles to the faces of dealers and customers.

The principal modification made to the first Cardinals was installation of inverted slots near the leading edge of the stabilator because it was discovered that in a full nose-up attitude, the stabilator was stalling out. This was Cessna's first application of a horizontal stabilator (which replaces the more conventional horizontal stabilizer and elevators) and it was chosen for the Cardinal because with the wing placed so far back for improved pilot visibility and better balance, tail surfaces would have had to be considerably enlarged or the fuselage lengthened to achieve adequate control using a stabilizer and elevator system. The stabilator is more effective for its size and saves both weight and drag.

TRENDSETTER

When the Cardinal first appeared, a Cessna engineer told us that it represented an engineering attempt to design the airplane of the seventies; a plane that would set

1971 Cardinal

the trend at Cessna for the coming decade. That was in the fall of 1967; and two years later, when the 1970 Model was announced, we believed that the Cardinal had evolved into that very thing. The 1969 Model went to 180-hp (from the original 150-hp); then the 1970 Model added a constant-speed propeller to efficiently employ those 30 extra horses, and also received an all-new wing (a new airfoil shape), a wing that at last made the sleek Cardinal "fly like a Cessna."

Then, obviously feeling that they had combined all the right things in a single airframe, Cessna coasted with the 1971 Model Cardinal and 177, offering no other significant changes except a redesigned nose-plate containing the landing light, plus some minor interior pretties. In 1975, the 177 landing gear was redesigned to provide an extra 7 mph in speed. From 1976 to 1978, the avionics and panel underwent various improvements, and in 1978, the fixed-gear 177s were dropped in favor of competing models.

About 1,000 of the original 1968 Models (150-hp) were built, and slightly over 400 of the 180-hp 1969 Cardinals followed. Despite hopes for an expanding post-recession market, the number of sales actually declined, remaining within about the 200-unit-per-year range until production ceased. In the used airplane marketplace, interest in this aircraft has, if anything, risen, and there is a strong Cardinal club for owners.

Going back to the tapes we made when we were introduced to the first Cardinal, we're reminded that that caper was a magazine assignment and, looking for a fresh angle to interest the reader, we invited a 20-year-old lady pilot, Miss Saundra Nix, to go along and do most of the flying so she could give her impressions. Sandy, a flight instructor, was a sophomore at Oklahoma State University at the time; she had soloed at 16 and obtained her commercial license at 18.

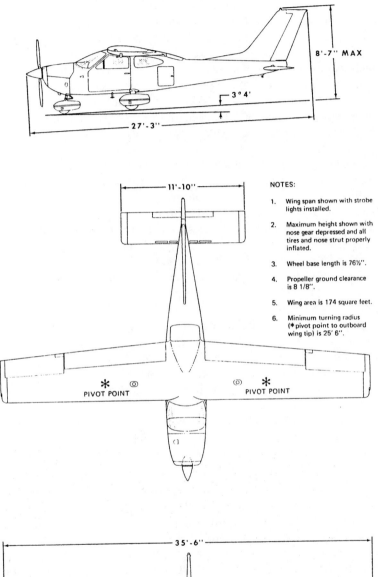

NOTES:

1. Wing span shown with strobe lights installed.

2. Maximum height shown with nose gear depressed and all tires and nose strut properly inflated.

3. Wheel base length is 76½".

4. Propeller ground clearance is 8 1/8".

5. Wing area is 174 square feet.

6. Minimum turning radius (* pivot point to outboard wing tip) is 25' 6".

1978 Cardinal views

INSTRUCTOR'S IMPRESSIONS

Sandy had been instructing in 150s, and was enchanted with the Cardinal's sports-car look, wide wheel-tread and its soft ground ride (this was Cessna's first use of the shot-peened vanadium-steel tubular gear legs). The plane's cabin was "huge" in Sandy's estimation, and so comfortable it was "unreal."

With Sandy flying and the checkpilot in the right-front seat, we had the spacious back seat to ourselves. So, we kept the tape recorder going and took notes on instrument readings in all flight regimes. Liftoff was normal, requiring eleven seconds and about 900 feet. We had a 3–5 knot south wind, ground temp of 80 degrees F, and were approximately 300 lbs under allowable gross. Sandy stayed low until we were clear of the McConnell AFB jet pattern, then climbed at 90 mph, which resulted in 800 fpm, dropping to about 700 fpm as we passed through 4,000 feet. There, she tried some stalls, which the Cardinal resisted with a noticeable buffet, sort of like a V-tail Bonanza, but recovery was quick and sure and Sandy reported that the airplane "felt good" throughout the stall. She also remarked that the variation between indicated airspeed and calibrated airspeed at high angles of attack seemed very small. This machine was supposed to stall at 64 mph without power and no flaps, and that's about what it indicated, instead of 55 or other low figure.

Cruise, at 75 percent power at 9,000 feet, was listed in the pilot's manual at 134 mph, and Zero Seven Yankee gave us 135 mph TAS under those conditions. Sandy remarked upon the effectiveness of the stabilator and fiddled with the trim, adding that this airplane "doesn't feel much like a 172."

At this point, we were approaching Eldorado, Kansas, so we went down to try some landings. Sandy was over the fence indicating 85 mph and she got a fair bounce at touchdown. She looked at the checkpilot as if he'd betrayed her. "I never bounce a Cessna with that old slab-steel gear on it," she accused.

"You overcontrolled a little," he replied. "Most people do until they get used to the new stabilator."

"Yecch!" Sandy said, sticking out her tongue. She fed-in power and went around for another try.

TUBULAR TESTIMONY

After her third landing—by then coming over the fence with 80 mph indicated—Sandy was putting the Cardinal down very nicely, so she abandoned the concrete runway and began shooting landings crosswind in the grass. The Cardinal's low profile proved very useful as well as pretty in this activity and our pilot reported that it handled a sidewind almost as well as a low-winger. And it was during the landings and takeoffs on the sod that we decided that Cessna should go to the new tubular-steel landing gear on all their airplanes. That ground was anything but smooth, but we got a smooth ground roll nevertheless, while the gear legs danced frantically in all directions. Truly, that new Cessna gear was the greatest thing since varnished propellers.

It was almost dark when we returned to Cessna Field, and by then Sandy was much taken with the Cardinal. Climbing into her little Cessna 150, she looked back at the shiny, low-slung Cardinal and sighed, "Now I know how Cinderella felt when her lovely coach turned back into a pumpkin."

In our view, the original Cardinal wasn't as unforgiving as some have claimed. If you were paying attention and flew it by feel instead of by rote, it behaved exactly as it was supposed to. What it failed to do was respond perfectly to Skyhawk technique because it simply was not just a strutless Skyhawk. We know a fellow out in Amarillo, Texas, who owns an early Cardinal and likes it. He says he's at a loss to explain why its original owner sold it at a bargain. We think the explanation might lie in the fact that our Texas friend had not been flying a Cessna when he bought his Cardinal.

Anyway, the 1970 and 1971 models of the Cardinal and 177 (the latter being the economy version of the Cardinal) have that new wing and a domesticated stabilator (modified linkage to the control wheel), and these changes, along with the extra power and constant-speed prop, do make this a different airplane—as Cessna said, a good airplane made great.

YEARLY IMPROVEMENTS

The 1971 model is a slightly fancied-up version of the '70 model with no significant aerodynamic change. The interior was restyled and padding added to door posts, front seat backs, and lower instrument panel. The wheel pants were reshaped again, which appears to be Cessna's way of keeping up with Detroit, and the nose-plate was redesigned to contain the landing light. All the good things were kept from previous models, of course, including the four-foot-wide doors that provide the easiest cabin entry and exit in the industry, and the 115-cubic-foot cabin remains the biggest in its class, offering posh surroundings for four adults and two children, or four people and lots of luggage. The 1971 Cardinal had a list of $17,995 and the Model 177 was priced at $16,795 fly-away-factory, Wichita.

The 1972 Cardinal possessed detail changes only, and few of those. The 1973 model appeared with a recontoured engine cowl and new model of the 180-hp Lycoming O-360 engine, which featured an improved oil filter system and a few pounds less weight. Maximum (optional) fuel capacity was upped to 61 gallons.

In 1974, the principal improvement to the Cardinal appears to have been a larger coat hanger in the baggage compartment. However, factory list price was held at the 1972 level.

By 1975, increased use of bonded construction in the doors and engine cowling, along with improved streamlining of the landing gear, had added a little speed.

The 1976 Cardinal could boast an even dozen changes, if you want to count such details as chrome-plated seat adjustment handles and stronger vent-window frame.

FIXED-GEAR FINALE

Final year of production for the fixed-gear Cardinal was 1978.

Factory price for 1978 was $49,975 as it rolled from the paint shop; in 1992, a good condition 1978 Cardinal would bring about $38,000 on the used market. The used value for Cardinals has not quite kept up with that of other aircraft, possibly because of their reputation for not handling like a true Cessna. The insider opinion is that this makes them a real bargain.

Popular modifications include STOL conversions, and a 180-hp/constant-speed prop conversion for improved performance. ADs are relatively few and include several engine items, a flap system change requirement (68-7-9), and a quick-drain modification requirement.

The Cardinal RG is discussed in chapter 11.

Table 6-1. 1978 Cardinal Classic performance & specifications.

SPEED:

Maximum at Sea Level	139 knots
Cruise, 75% Power at 10,000 Ft	130 knots

CRUISE: *Recommended lean mixture with fuel allowance for engine start, taxi, takeoff, climb and 45 minutes reserve at 45% power.*

75% Power at 10,000 Ft	*Range*	535 nm
49 Gallons Usable Fuel	*Time*	4.2 hrs
75% Power at 10,000 Ft	*Range*	675 nm
60 Gallons Usable Fuel	*Time*	5.3 hrs
Maximum Range at 10,000 Ft	*Range*	615 nm
49 Gallons Usable Fuel	*Time*	6.1 hrs
Maximum Range at 10,000 Ft	*Range*	780 nm
60 Gallons Usable Fuel	*Time*	7.7 hrs

RATE OF CLIMB AT SEA LEVEL   840 fpm

SERVICE CEILING   14,600 ft

TAKEOFF PERFORMANCE:

Ground Roll	750 ft
Total Distance Over 50-Ft Obstacle	1400 ft

LANDING PERFORMANCE:

Ground Roll	600 ft
Total Distance Over 50-Ft Obstacle	1220 ft

STALL SPEED (CAS):

Flaps Up, Power Off	55 knots
Flaps Down, Power Off	46 knots

MAXIMUM WEIGHT   2500 lbs

STANDARD EMPTY WEIGHT   1643 lbs

MAXIMUM USEFUL LOAD   857 lbs

BAGGAGE ALLOWANCE   120 lbs

WING LOADING: *Pounds/Sq Ft*   14.4

POWER LOADING: *Pounds/HP*   13.9

FUEL CAPACITY: *Total*

Standard Tanks	50 gal
Long Range Tanks	61 gal

OIL CAPACITY   9 qts

ENGINE: *Avco Lycoming*   O-360-A1F6D
180 BHP at 2700 RPM

PROPELLER: *Constant Speed, Diameter*   76 in

7

Cessna 150 and 152

CESSNA DID NOT MANUFACTURE a two-place airplane for seven years after the last Cessna 140A left the assembly line in Wichita on February 23, 1951; however, by 1958, a good two-place trainer was so much in demand that flight operators were paying more for seven-year-old 140s than those craft sold for new. True, a couple of good fabric-covered two-placers were on the market, but the economical all-metal 140A had spoiled a lot of flight operators and customers; nothing less than a 140 follow-on would do.

Happily, Cessna listened to those voices from the aeronautical wilderness and produced a 140 follow-on. They called it the Cessna 150.

The first 150 appeared late in 1958, and it did not pretend to improve upon the 140's performance figures, but instead used its ten extra horsepower to do much the same with greater ease and comfort without significantly increasing cost of operation. In short, it was a scaled-down 172, and except for the pleasant fact that the new 150 had a slightly quicker control response—seemed a bit more "lighthearted"—it inherited all of the 172's amiable characteristics. It came close to being the ideal sport/trainer, as its apparently ageless popularity has attested ever since.

Now, before we go any further we must acknowledge that a lot of people might protest the above statement. Some will maintain that the ideal sport/trainer is the Cherokee 140; others will say it's the Musketeer Sport or the Citabria . . .. Therefore, we've got to hedge by admitting that it all depends upon who's talking. It isn't possible to honestly say that one airplane is "better" than another because every aircraft design is a compromise; to get something, you have to give something. If you want speed, for example, you must pay for it with other desirable traits, including economy of operation. So, the most anyone can do is decide which airplane is best for him; and that, clearly, is determined by each individual's preferences, prejudices and, perhaps, the personal weaknesses most of us possess. But we can allow our "ideal" statement to stand if we add "for the most people," because the Cessna 150 has far outsold all other planes in its class.

1966 C-150F (Author's airplane.)

POPULAR TRAINER

In 1969, 61 percent of all flight-training hours were flown in Cessnas, primarily the 150. Of the 6.8 million flight-training hours flown that year in the U.S. by all types of aircraft, 3.1 million flight-training hours were accounted for by the Cessna 150. So, who can argue with success of that magnitude?

The 1962 and 1963 Models (Commuter version) had low empty weights, and slightly better performance. The big rear window was added in 1964; doors were enlarged and squared-off and the swept-rudder added in 1966. The conical-camber wingtips came with the 1970 Model, and in 1971 the 150 received that lovely tubular-steel landing gear, new noseplate with landing light and extended prop shaft, plus new dorsal fin, and, of course, reshaped wheel pants (called "speed fairings" by Cessna advertising men, though they add little speed).

The conical wingtips, which improve turn and slow-flight stability, are about the only significant aerodynamic changes in the 150 design since its inception. All the other many improvements have made it quieter, easier to handle on the ground, handier to operate in the air, better to see out of, and prettier to look at.

The 150 was retired in 1977, and the 152 was introduced in 1978. The 152 featured a number of significant changes along with a different engine, but retained the same basic airframe.

The first 150, the 1959 Model, is still a nice little flying machine if it has been properly maintained (we probably should speak of all Cessna models in present tense because all—back through the pre-World War-II Airmaster—are still flying in surprising numbers). The 1959 Model has the pull-starter (since replaced by the key ignition), and a cabin more closely resembling the 140 than that of later 150's; but it flies just like its fancier offspring of later years.

GOOD VALUE

One of these early ones, say, 1959–1963, which may be found in the used plane market at prices ranging from $7,000 to $9,000, is probably a much better buy than the cheaper, fabric-covered used planes for the median-income pilot who flies mostly for fun. The 150 will not depreciate much—in fact, given the current mar-

1978 C-152 II

Robert B. Slobins/Phototake

ket, inflation, and a lack of new trainers, the price of used 150s has been rising swiftly. Its maintenance will be less costly, particularly if one is faced with a re-cover job on the rag-winger. Also, the 150 is always good merchandise in the used market when one is ready to trade or sell. During the late sixties, it was not at all uncommon for a man to buy a used 150, fly it for a couple of years, then sell it for as much as he paid for it in the first place. His cost of ownership was represented by whatever it cost him to keep it in top condition. And because the average 150 (all models) will burn only 5 to 6 gallons of fuel per hour (at 115–120 mph), it gives compact-car gas mileage.

In the 1990s, it is actually possible to buy a used 150, fly it for a couple of years, then sell it at a profit. Normal ownership costs are then partially offset, making the 150 even cheaper to own.

But, "practical" reasons aside, the 150 also has a sort of friendly air about it that just naturally attracts people. In contrast to the rather ominous stance of the bigger, faster, and more powerful craft that seems to challenge you to flight, the saucy little 150 invites you with a twinkle, as if to say, "C'mon, let's go have some fun . . .."

This characteristic implies, of course, that it won't place any great demands upon you. And it doesn't. We taped a demonstration ride in a 1966 Model—that was the year the swept rudder and bigger doors were added, along with larger tire size (same as 172)—and this airplane, with a little over 1,100 hours on its record-ing tach, still looked new late in 1970.

INNOVATIONS

We were surprised to discover that the old pull-type starter lever was still used in the 150 as late as 1966, and the flap indicator, above the left window, was awk-ward to read; but electric flaps began with this model and the old "axe handle" flap lever disappeared from between the seats in favor of a switch on the panel. Stabilizer trim is on a console just below the throttle.

1986 C-152

To start the engine, mixture is set at "Rich," fuel selector switch, "On" (there are no Left and Right positions for individual fuel tanks), crack throttle ¼ inch, a couple of shots of primer, clear the prop, and firmly pull the starter T-handle.

As the oil pressure comes up, we ask Ground Control at Lawton (Oklahoma) Municipal for taxi instructions and then move out. She rolls easily, the 100-hp Continental muttering happily under its breath. Nosewheel steering with the rudder pedals is quick and positive. On the taxi strip, we set altimeter (field elevation, 1,108 ft), and determine that we are about 170 lbs below our allowable gross weight.

Prior to takeoff, the magneto checks are made at 1,700 rpms. The Owner's Manual discourages full-power run-ups unless a malfunction is suspected. Besides, with plenty of runway available, the full-power check is more practical during the early part of the takeoff run because there's plenty of room to shut down everything and stop if a problem is suspected. Completing our pretakeoff check, we make sure the doors are latched; all flight controls free; adjust stabilizer trim to "Takeoff;" check operation of carburetor heat (leaving it at "Cold"), and check flaps in "Up" position. Then, with tower's blessing, we feed in power and accelerate down the runway centerline.

As the air speed passes 40 mph, we begin to ease back on the control wheel and a few seconds later, as the airspeed needle passes 50 mph, the 150 is off. We leave the engine at full power and adjust the speed at 85 mph with the control wheel. This results in an initial climb rate of 650 feet per minute (fpm) with an OAT of 64 degrees F. A steeper angle, which brings the airspeed needle back to 75 mph, gives us 740 fpm. We leave the pattern and continue upward on a westerly heading to get away from military and airline traffic in the area.

CRUISE 115 MPH TRUE

We lean mixture as we climb to maintain best rpms, and level off at 5,000 feet, which puts us well above the haze layer in clear air. A check on cruising speeds at

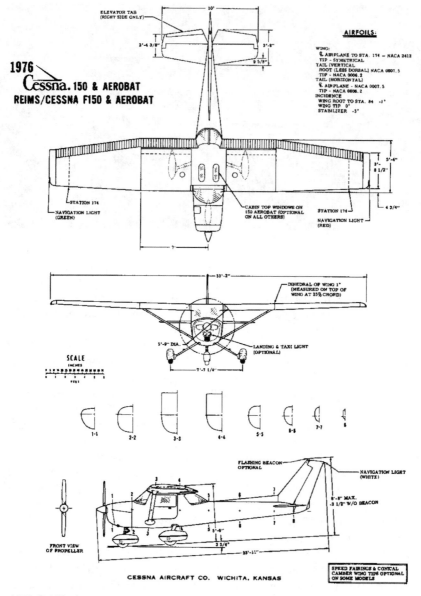

CESSNA AIRCRAFT CO. WICHITA, KANSAS

1960 C-150 views

this altitude shows 121 mph TAS turning 2,750 rpms. It drops back to about 108 mph TAS at 2,500 rpms. This latter setting should reduce fuel consumption to about 5 gph (from more than 6 gph) and increase range by approximately 75 miles. It is also, of course, easier on the engine. Optimum cruise at 2,650 rpms produces 115 mph true at this height.

We try some stalls, and with power off and no flaps, the 150 mushes along, control wheel back, wings level at 48 mph IAS. With flaps down and power off,

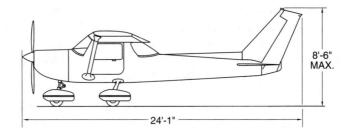

8'-6" MAX.

24'-1"

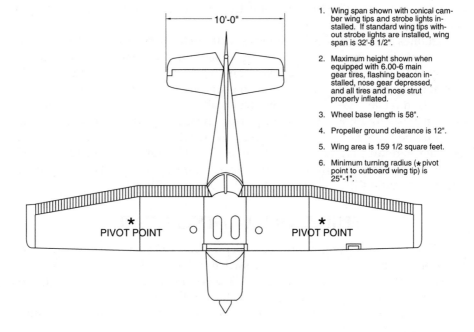

10'-0"

★ PIVOT POINT

★ PIVOT POINT

1. Wing span shown with conical camber wing tips and strobe lights installed. If standard wing tips without strobe lights are installed, wing span is 32'-8 1/2".

2. Maximum height shown when equipped with 6.00-6 main gear tires, flashing beacon installed, nose gear depressed, and all tires and nose strut properly inflated.

3. Wheel base length is 58".

4. Propeller ground clearance is 12".

5. Wing area is 159 1/2 square feet.

6. Minimum turning radius (★ pivot point to outboard wing tip) is 25"-1".

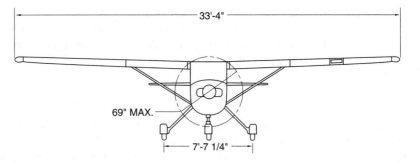

33'-4"

69" MAX.

7'-7 1/4"

1985 C-152 views

there is a more definite break at about 42 mph IAS, preceded by some buffeting, but again, wings remain level and the airplane is flying almost as soon as back pressure on the wheel is relaxed. It's a little more fun stalling out of a 30-degree bank with flaps. The break is quite clean from this attitude and the buffeting pronounced, while the pay-off comes at about 58 mph. However, the down-wing comes up at once and recovery is swift.

The only surprise one is likely to encounter doing stalls in the later model Cessnas (beginning with the 1966 Model 150), is the weird sound (our colleague Don Downie likened it to the "dying gasp of a collapsing bag pipe") of the Cessna pneumatic reed stall-warning device. This system, maintenance-free and nonelectrical, admits the relative wind through a ¾-inch opening in the wing's leading edge; the air flows through the reed device to produce an increasingly eerie sound as one approaches the stall. It really raises the hair on the back of your neck and should be the most effective stall-warner in the business, next to a short-tempered flight instructor.

Landings are typical Cessna landings. You can make the 150 float and porpoise coming in with too much speed and a high flare, but it'll eventually mush onto the runway and land itself anyway. Or, you can drag over the fence at 60 mph and plop it down firmly on all three wheels. It won't complain. But if you're willing to work at your landings a little, this airplane will really make you look good in the maneuver that has traditionally been the primary measuring stick of pilot proficiency.

From the time the first 150 appeared late in 1958, it was offered in three versions, the Standard, Trainer, and Commuter. The 150 Aerobat was added in 1970, and about 300 were sold during its first year in production. (Still another version is the French-built F150, sold throughout Europe since 1966.)

TUBULAR LANDING GEAR

The 1971 Model 150s were announced in September, 1970, and the most significant improvement (in our opinion) was the switch to the Cardinal-type hollow, tubular-steel gear legs. This system gives the 150 an even wider track, nearly 8 ft, and a ground ride that surely can't be bettered short of the hovercraft principle. If that isn't enough, Cessna says that this gear has four to five times the service life of previous landing gears.

Interiors were again poshed-up for '71, and the contoured cabin ceiling of easy-to-clean, rip-resistant Ensolite (a 1970 innovation) added 2½ inches to headroom. A new level of quietness resulted from the propeller extension and new cowling. There was also a new safety belt system. Few further changes were made until the final production year of 1977.

AEROBAT

The Cessna 150 Aerobat is the versatile one. It is a trainer, cross-country personal/business plane, and a fun machine approved for all the aerobatic maneuvers most private pilots are likely to master. It is certified for barrel rolls, aileron rolls, single snap rolls, loops, Immelmann turns, spins, Cuban-8s, and vertical reversements. It is stressed for six Gs positive and three Gs negative flight loads. Special equipment includes quick-release door mechanisms, seats with removable bottom and back cushions to accommodate either back or seat-pack parachutes, quick-release lap belts and shoulder harness, tinted ceiling skylights, and G-meter, plus the distinctive paint job.

We used to visit the late akro champ Hal Krier whenever we were in Wichita because aerobatics had fascinated us ever since those long-ago days when we dared a loop or two with the Spartan C-3 bipe in which we got our first bootleg stick-time (with a 40-hour newly-minted private pilot acting as our instructor). And when the 150 Aerobat appeared, we hoped we'd be lucky enough to get Krier to fly with us and put it through its paces.

We weren't that lucky, but we were fortunate enough to be in Wichita the day Harold Krier (three-time Men's National Champion Aerobatic Pilot) evaluated the prototype 150 Aerobat back in June, 1969. We had dinner with Harold that evening (actually, hamburgers and malts at a drive-in) and he was enthusiastic over the new Aerobat.

Harold told us that, in his opinion, this craft represented an excellent blending of desirable traits in a sport/trainer: capable of all the fancy didoes the average private pilot has any business performing; yet it retained all the forgiving and gentle qualities of its noncheckered sisters. In fact, it was the same as other 150s, with just a little beefing-up here and there.

Harold said he had performed snap rolls; snaps from wingovers, slow rolls, 4-point rolls (without power), Immelmanns, loops, loops with snaps, Cuban-8s, spins, and a number of inverted maneuvers that the airplane would not be certified for. He said the rudder was inadequate for some maneuvers, but explained that that is true of almost any production craft not designed exclusively for aerobatics.

Harold did surprise us when he said he hoped Cessna kept the 100-hp engine in the Aerobat; we had always had the impression that the tumble types wanted power to spare. But Krier said, "I think the 150 is a very nice little package as it stands, and I don't think Cessna should tamper with it. Give it a bigger engine and you have to modify the airframe. It gets bigger and heavier and more expensive and you no longer have a 150, but something else entirely."

INTERIOR RECONFIGURATION

By 1972, the Cessna 150 alone accounted for 15 percent of all flying done. It's hard to add much to a recommendation of that caliber. It's even harder to significantly improve upon a machine that satisfies its market so well. The 1973 Model 150 appeared with lower seats for more headroom, and a redesigned instrument panel along with new control wheels.

The 1974 Cessna 150s gained little but cosmetic changes such as reshaped wheel fairings and of course a different paint scheme. The 1974 Aerobat was fitted with a propeller possessing a Clark Y airfoil section, and this increased cruising and top speeds to 119 and 124 mph respectively, while raising service ceiling to 14,000 ft.

The 1975 models of the 150 series received increased fin and rudder area for better crosswind handling by adding six inches to the height of the rudder. The extra rudder is especially useful to the Aerobat model because, as any aerobatic pilot will tell you, no production airplane ever has enough rudder for precision aerobatics. The Clark Y propeller, proven on the '74 Aerobat, was installed on all 150 models in 1975.

The new prop, along with the improved wheel and brake fairings, did add performance—up to 130 mph top speed with full throttle and the tach 200 rpms over redline. Actually, we got 119 mph TAS at a more practical 2,650 rpms.

The 1976 models of the 150 series offered little improvement over the previous year—chromed door handles, slight amount of new soundproofing, and seats ground-adjustable for height. The 150 acquired a few ADs in its long history, but most should be complied with as a matter of course. Both the 150 and 152 have the seat rail item, issued for most models; it isn't too difficult or expensive to get fixed. The 150 also had a 1,000-hour nosegear fork inspection requirement, and some models need new wing attachment fittings (73-23-7). The 152 has a few engine items (check your model and year), a few flap and aileron items, and a heater muffler inspection or replacement AD.

The 1976 factory suggested prices: $12,650 for the Standard 150; $16,350 for the 150 Commuter; $18,750 for the Commuter II with complete avionics, and $15,250 for the Aerobat.

Just two years later, 1978, the 152 replaced the 150. It primarily represented a change from the Continental engine that took 80 octane low-lead gas to a 100 octane Lycoming O-235-L2C engine. Other changes included a switch to the 28-volt electrical system used on other models, a new McCauley propeller design, and a switch from the 150's 40-degree flap maximum, to 30 degrees. Apart from this, and minor airframe changes to accommodate the new engine, the 152 is basically a 150 with slightly more power.

152

The 152, like the 150, is available in standard, commuter, trainer, and aerobat versions. A standard 1978 model 152, unequipped, went for $14,950 when new; this plane (good condition) could bring $17,000 to $20,000 on the used market, demonstrating the still strong market for late model trainers. The last 152 models were built in 1985–86.

The 152 flies a lot like the 150. Its characteristics are so similar, in fact, that you might not really notice the difference. The 152 does seem to pack a bit more punch—that's partly due to its larger engine, and partly due to the fact that 152s are certain to be younger than 150s. Many 150 pilots miss the 40 degrees of flaps; the 152 has only 30 degrees. When we "transitioned" from a 152 trainer to an owned 150, the only major thing to get used to was the pull starter (1966 model) and slight differences in locations of things. Fuel was not as much a problem as anticipated.

Due to its popularity and versatility, the 150 and 152 have a host of popular modifications available. Among these mods are taildragger conversion, an engine upgrade to 150, 160, or even 180 hp, long-range tanks, STOL kits, and wingtips.

Table 7-1. 1976 C-150/A150 performance & specifications.

	Commuter		Aerobat	
SPEED:				
Maximum at Sea Level	109 knots	202 kph	108 knots	200 kph
Cruise, 75% Power at 7000 Ft	106 knots	196 kph	105 knots	194 kph
CRUISE: *Recommended Lean Mixture with fuel allowance for engine start, taxi, takeoff, climb and 45 minutes reserve at 45% power.*				
75% Power at 7000 Ft with	340 nm	630 km	335 nm	620 km
22.5 Gallons Usable Fuel	3.3 hr	3.3 hr	3.3 hr	3.3 hr
75% Power at 7000 Ft with	580 nm	1074 km	570 nm	1086 km
35 Gallons Usable Fuel	5.5 hr	5.5 hr	5.5 hr	5.5 hr
Maximum Range at 10,000 Ft with	420 nm	778 km	415 nm	769 km
22.5 Gallons Usable Fuel	4.9 hr	4.9 hr	4.9 hr	4.9 hr
Maximum Range at 10,000 Ft with	735 nm	1361 km	725 nm	1343 km
35 Gallons Usable Fuel	8.5 hr	8.5 hr	8.5 hr	8.5 hr
RATE OF CLIMB AT SEA LEVEL	670 fpm	204 mpm	670 fpm	204 mpm
SERVICE CEILING	14,000 ft	4267 m	14,000 ft	4267 m
TAKEOFF PERFORMANCE:				
Ground Roll	735 ft	224 m	735 ft	224 m
Total Distance Over 50-Ft Obstacle	1385 ft	422 m	1385 ft	422 m
LANDING PERFORMANCE:				
Ground Roll	445 ft	136 m	445 ft	136 m
Total Distance Over 50-Ft Obstacle	1075 ft	328 m	1075 ft	328 m
STALL SPEED (IAS):				
Flaps Up, Power Off	46 knots	85 kph	49 knots	91 kph
Flaps Down, Power Off	42 knots	78 kph	44 knots	82 kph
MAXIMUM WEIGHT	1600 lbs	726 kg	1600 lb	726 kg
STANDARD EMPTY WEIGHT:				
Commuter/Aerobat	1104 lb	501 kg	1076 lb	488 kg
Commuter II	1122 lb	509 kg	—	—
MAXIMUM USEFUL LOAD:				
Commuter/Aerobat	496 lb	225 kg	524 lb	238 kg
Commuter II	478 lb	217 kg	—	—
BAGGAGE ALLOWANCE	120 lb	54 kg	120 lb	54 kg
WING LOADING	10.0 lb/sq ft	48.9 kg/sq m	10.2 lb/sq ft	49.8 kg/sq m
POWER LOADING	16.0 lb/hp	7.3 kg/hp	16.0 lb/hp	7.3 kg/hp
WING SPAN	33 ft, 2 in	10.11 m	32 ft, 8½ in	9.97 m
WING AREA	159.5 sq ft	14.8 sq m	157 sq ft	14.6 sq m
LENGTH	23 ft, 11 in	7.29 m	23 ft, 11 in	7.29 m
HEIGHT	8 ft, 6 in	2.59 m	8 ft, 6 in	2.59 m
FUEL CAPACITY, *Total:*				
Standard Tanks	26 gal	98 liters	26 gal	98 liters
Long Range Tanks	38 gal	144 liters	38 gal	144 liters
OIL CAPACITY	6 qt	5.7 liters	6 qt	5.7 liters
ENGINE	Teledyne Continental O-200-A Engine; 100 bhp at 2750 rpm			
PROPELLER	Fixed Pitch, 69 inch diameter (1.75 m)			

Table 7-2. 1985 C-152 performance & specifications.

SPEED:

Maximum at Sea Level		110 knots
Cruise, 75% Power at 8000 Ft		107 knots

CRUISE: Recommended lean mixture with fuel allowance for engine start, taxi, takeoff, climb and 45 minutes reserve at 45% power.

75% Power at 8000 Ft	Range	350 nm
24.5 Gallons Usable Fuel	Time	3.4 hrs
75% Power at 8000 Ft	Range	580 nm
37.5 Gallons Usable Fuel	Time	5.5 hrs
Maximum Range at 10,000 Ft	Range	415 nm
24.5 Gallons Usable Fuel	Time	5.2 hrs
Maximum Range at 10,000 Ft	Range	690 nm
37.5 Gallons Usable Fuel	Time	8.7 hrs

RATE OF CLIMB AT SEA LEVEL — 715 fpm

SERVICE CEILING — 14,700 ft

TAKEOFF PERFORMANCE:

Ground Roll	725 ft
Total Distance Over 50-Ft Obstacle	1340 ft

LANDING PERFORMANCE:

Ground Roll	475 ft
Total Distance Over 50-Ft Obstacle	1200 ft

STALL SPEED (CAS):

Flaps Up, Power Off	48 knots
Flaps Down, Power Off	43 knots

MAXIMUM WEIGHT — 1670 lbs

STANDARD EMPTY WEIGHT:

152	1081 lbs
152 II	1118 lbs

MAXIMUM USEFUL LOAD:

152	589 lbs
152 II	552 lbs

BAGGAGE ALLOWANCE — 120 lbs

WING LOADING: Pounds/Sq Ft — 10.5

POWER LOADING: Pounds/HP — 15.2

FUEL CAPACITY: Total

Standard Tanks	26 gal
Long Range Tanks	39 gal

OIL CAPACITY — 6 qts

ENGINE: Avco Lycoming — O-235-L2C
110 BHP at 2550 RPM

PROPELLER: Fixed Pitch, Diameter — 69 in

8

Cessna 182s and 205

THE CESSNA 182 APPEARED IN 1956. It was a Model 180 with tricycle landing gear. Except for styling differences, the same could be said for the 182s and Skylanes (the Skylane is the posh version of the 182) built through 1971. The 182/Skylane represents a substantial step upward from the 172/Skyhawk series, and the transition is not lightly made because the Skylane does not fly or land like a Skyhawk. It's five hundred pounds more airplane, with more power efficiently applied via a constant-speed prop, and it insists that its new owner stops grinning and starts thinking. It's not a student airplane; it's for serious cross-country transportation—any kind of country.

Because we didn't have a 1971 Model Skylane handy, we took a demonstration ride in a '69 Model. There was little change in this craft from 1969–72, except for a slight weight increase; we were surprised that the '71 did not switch to tubular-steel gear legs. The demo ride didn't turn out very well because we had only a couple of hours to go on a raw November day. That was decidedly unfair to an airplane that likes to get up high and go far. Our veteran Cessna man at Lawton (Oklahoma) Municipal, Ray Johnson, says that no one can really appreciate the Skylane until he's taken it on a long cross-country flight, preferably to California or Oregon and back with some stops at high-altitude airports in the West.

As we said, the first (1956) 182 was a 180 with tricycle landing gear. In 1957, the gear legs were shortened, and a year later the Skylane version appeared. The swept tail was added in 1960; in '61 came an additional window on each side, and in 1962 the big rear window for 360-degree vision, plus electric flaps and a wider cabin. A lot of interior improvements followed during the next five years, then the 1969 Model again had its main gear legs shortened and the space between the wheels expanded. But because the nosewheel could not be lowered (due to the need for prop clearance with the ground), this resulted in a slightly nose-high stance for the 182/Skylane, a situation that makes for easier entry and exit from the cabin, perhaps better rough-field handling, and a lower profile to better handle crosswind landings. But it doesn't do anything for the pilot transitioning from the 172 because if he drives the 182 down to land like some people do the super-

1986 Skylane

car, he's liable to bend the firewall a little. The 182/Skylane must be brought in for a nose-high touchdown on the main wheels.

Of course, the 182 pilots will be quick to point out that that's the way we should have been landing the 172 and 150 (experienced flyers are like reformed sinners; they have small tolerance for those of us who are doing things the way they used to).

NOT A 172

Anyway, the point is, the 182/Skylane is not going to cover up for you or shrug off indifferent control handling. She steps higher than the 172 and requires a tighter rein.

This is not to say that the Skylane is hard to fly or tricky. It isn't. It's still a Cessna. But the controls are heavier and you know you're flying more airplane. The principal differences for the pilot stepping up from the 150 or 172 will probably be in landings and power management. That "extra throttle"—prop control—gives fresh significance to the tachometer and adds a manifold pressure gauge.

Engine starting procedure is much like that of the 172 except that you have cowl flaps to open and prop pitch control to push in for "High rpms." The pretakeoff runup is done at the usual 1,700 rpms (with prop in high rpms), and in addition, you'll "exercise" the prop a couple of times—pull out the knob, changing pitch from high to low rpms—to ensure oil circulation that activates pitch change. Then, leaving the prop in high rpms, feed in full throttle for takeoff.

You'll notice the extra power, and 60 mph will come quickly. You'll also notice that it requires a firmer pressure to lift the nosewheel off if you've been flying a Skyhawk.

1978 Skylane RG

Maximum power for the takeoff climb should be limited to that absolutely necessary for safety, according to the Skylane Owner's Manual, so we reduce power to the recommended 23 inches of manifold pressure and 2,450 rpms (about 75 percent power) for climbout at 100 mph. This gives us 1,300 fpm with the OAT registering 44 degrees F. We are almost 50 lbs light, however. The book says we can get 1,700 fpm at this loading with full power and an IAS of 85 mph.

CRUISE AND RANGE FLEXIBILITY

The Skylane gives quite a bit of flexibility in cruise and range at various altitudes. Fully loaded, at 2,500 feet, turning 2,450 with 23 inches, TAS is 156 mph and range (with 60 gal) is 660 miles. This can be stretched to 865 miles at this inefficient altitude if you cut rpms to 2,000 and manifold pressure to 17 inches with a TAS of 100 mph. But you aren't likely to ever go anywhere at that altitude in a Skylane. Seventy-five hundred feet is much better; 10,000 is probably best, and you can go to 15,000 if you have oxygen. At 15,000, 2,450 rpms and 16 inches will give you 145 mph TAS and a range of 835 miles.

For a given throttle setting, select the lowest rpms (with the prop control) in the green arc range that will give smooth engine operation. Cowl flaps should be adjusted to maintain cylinder head temperature at approximately ⅔ of the normal operating range (green arc); and to lean the mixture for the best range, pull out the mixture control until the engine becomes rough, then push it back in just far enough to smooth out the engine again. Any change in altitude, power setting, or carburetor heat will require a change in the lean mixture setting.

It's possible to land the Skylane without use of trim, but that's doing it the hard way. And although the book says to bring it in power-off with 40-degrees of flap at 69 mph for short-field landings, this produces a fairly high sink rate and

1964 C-205A

you've got to be right on top of it to make your flare just right or you'll touch down pretty hard. Seems to us the best way is to hold a little power and flatten out the final, gradually backing off the throttle and closing it just a little before flare. Then hold the wheel well back to ensure that you touch down on the main gear. It's best to hold the nosewheel off for the first couple of hundred feet of the rollout, unless you have a crosswind to contend with.

TUBULAR LANDING GEAR

The 1970 Model 182/Skylane adopted the conical cambered wingtips and new elevator control system to lower elevator stick forces. Improvements from 1970 to 1977: tubular landing gear added, an extended dorsal fin was offered, an oxygen system was made available, and the landing lights were moved from the wing to the front. The 1977 model also offered a higher compression 100-octane Continental O-470-U engine.

In 1979, fuel capacity was increased in the standard version. Apart from the introduction of turbocharged and retractable gear models, no other major changes were made up to the 1986 final production year. Basic list price of the 1986 182 was $80,950, the Skylane, slightly higher. Used prices range from about $100,000 for a 1986 model all the way down to about $20,000 for an early Model 182.

A number of interesting modifications have been made through the years, including long-range tanks, baggage compartment tanks, wing tips, STOL kits, and a recently introduced streamlined gear conversion offered by Horton, Inc. ADs include the usual seat rail item, a few engine items, an aileron hinge item, and requirement to replace wing attachment fittings. Like the 180, the 182 also has several ADs regarding fuel cells; specifically, that the cells tend to get wrinkled and store water, so quick drains and a 12-month inspection are required (84-10-1).

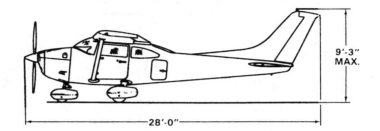

9'-3"
MAX.

28'-0"

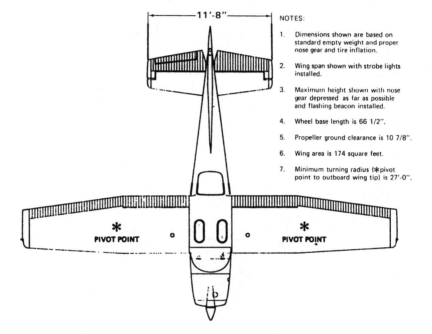

11'-8"

NOTES:

1. Dimensions shown are based on standard empty weight and proper nose gear and tire inflation.

2. Wing span shown with strobe lights installed.

3. Maximum height shown with nose gear depressed as far as possible and flashing beacon installed.

4. Wheel base length is 66 1/2".

5. Propeller ground clearance is 10 7/8".

6. Wing area is 174 square feet.

7. Minimum turning radius (✱pivot point to outboard wing tip) is 27'-0".

✱
PIVOT POINT

✱
PIVOT POINT

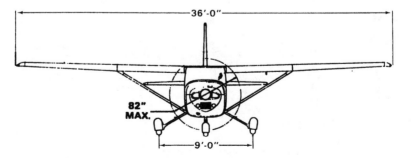

36'-0"

82"
MAX.

9'-0"

1986 Skylane (182R) views

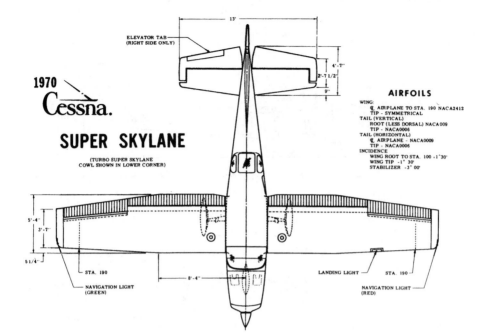

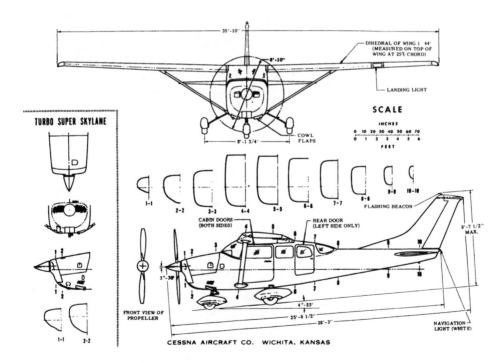

1970 Super Skylane views

SKYLANE RG

The retractable gear Skylane RG, model C-R182, was introduced in 1978. The RG version had a larger 235-hp Lycoming O-540-J3C5D engine. It also had a 28-volt electrical system, longer cowl, and a higher gross weight. This model got an increase in fuel capacity from 76 to 88 gallons in 1979. The last production year was 1986.

A 1986 Skylane RG cost $106,650 at standard retail, and fetches about $125,000 on the 1992 retail market.

TURBO SKYLANE RG

A turbocharged version of the C-R182 was introduced in 1979 as the Turbo Skylane RG. The CTR182, as it was designated, featured a 235 hp Lycoming O-540-L3C5D engine, with a turbocharger developed by AiResearch and Cessna. The fixed-gear Skylane appeared in a turbocharged version in 1981; it was designated the C-T182 Turbo Skylane. Production of these models ended in 1986, when Cessna single-engine airplane production ceased.

The 1986 Turbo Skylane RG that cost $118,500 standard retail is about $140,000 on the 1992 used market.

CESSNA 205

The Cessna 205 was produced from 1962–1964 inclusive. It has been described as a stretched Skylane with an additional 30-hp and fuel injection. It was also called, at the time it appeared, a Cessna 210 with fixed landing gear. Anyway, fewer than 600 were built during those three years before it was replaced by—or evolved into—the Super Skylane.

The Super Skylane and Turbo Super Skylane would be easier for Cessna watchers to fit into their proper categories if Cessna would only call them "Super 206s" instead of Skylanes because it seems to us these craft aren't really Skylanes, but a definite step upward—in power, size, and weight—to another class. They are in fact uptown versions of the 206 Skywagon. For the extra conveniences, snootier name and different paint scheme, you pay $1,400 ($25,995 for the '70 Skywagon 206 vs. $27,450 for the '70 Super Skylane), and this would seem to lend weight to our longstanding suspicion that Cessna dealers need only to ask, "How much money have you got?" in order to roll out an airplane and match that figure almost to the dollar. (We can just picture the scene: "But I've only got $27,406.09," the customer says. "That's all right, sir," the dealer replies and, picking up the phone, asks for his service department. "Okay, Mae, take a seat out of that new Super Skylane. A gentleman here wants a five-placer.")

Seriously, Cessna at one time covered the gen-av market in gradual steps, from the 150 to the Citation 500 jet.

AIR TAXI AIRPLANE

The Super Skylane was introduced late in 1964 (1965 Model), and was intended for the charter and air taxi operators. It would comfortably seat six adults (with plenty of leg room) and then take off with full tanks and nearly 200 lbs of luggage. At optimum altitude, it would haul this load nearly 600 miles (with reserve fuel) at 160 mph or better, and it would do so economically, its fuel-injected 285-hp Continental IO-520-A engine consuming about 15 gallons of gas per hour.

By 1970, the Super Skylane had gained 300 lbs at gross weight and had an increased useful load of 250 lbs—at the cost of a slight amount of speed/range/initial climb. It seemed an excellent airplane for its task, but its future appeared uncertain because the Cessna 207—for very little more money—could do even more with the same engine. In 1971, with a variety of upscale cosmetic changes, the Super Skylane was renamed the Stationair.

The Turbo Super Skylane, introduced in 1966, is equipped with a turbo supercharger. It has less useful load than its unboosted sister, but will get up high and go fast.

The supercharger helps the engine breathe more efficiently when the temperature is hot and the density altitude is high. It provides 32.5 inches of manifold pressure up to 19,000 ft. Above that, it keeps working like an extra set of lungs compressing the thin air into a richer source of oxygen for the engine. As a result, the Turbo Super Skylane can effectively operate off the highest airfields in the world fully loaded.

This airplane will climb out at 1,030 fpm initially and has a minimum loss of horsepower as altitude is gained. The turbo system continues to deliver cruise power up to 24,000 ft. There are no continuous control or throttle adjustments during climb and no additional gauges to watch. The fuel-injected, 285-hp Continental engine (TSI0-520-C) is specially adapted for turbocharging, and the turbine is automatically regulated by an absolute pressure controller and overboost control valve.

OXYGEN STANDARD

A two- or three-hour oxygen system is standard equipment on the Turbo Super Skylane. This installation includes an overhead console with capacity gauge and system control, six individual ports, control wheel microphone switch, external filler valve, and a 76-cubic-inch oxygen bottle.

Suggested list price of the Super Skylane for 1970 was $27,450. The Turbo Super Skylane for 1970 was priced at $31,950. The two models for the Super Skylane were discontinued after 1971; 649 were built and almost all are still flying. The 182 and Skylane continued in production until 1986; indeed, ranking third in sales behind the Skyhawk and 150/152 models.

The Skylane appeared with the new tubular steel landing gear and "Camber-Lift" wing in 1972, resulting in a softer ground ride and better slow flight characteristics. The wing leading edge was bonded, and this began the aerodynamic cleanup that added bonded doors and upper cowl in '73, new air scoops in '73, new engine baffles and Clark Y propeller section in '74, along with improved wheel and strut fairings and smoothed edges on fin and rudder in 1976. In 1977, 182Q version with a 230-hp Continental O-470-R engine was introduced. Along the way were a host of detail comfort/convenience changes, as well.

Factory price in 1982: $75,650 for the basic Skylane; $91,100 for the Turbo model; a 1986 retractable sold for $80,950. The 1992 used plane prices for these same models were $97,000, $110,000, and $108,000, respectively.

Table 8-1. 1986 Skylane (182R) performance & specifications.

SPEED:

Maximum at Sea Level		146 knots
Cruise, 75% Power at 8000 Ft		142 knots

CRUISE: *Recommended lean mixture with fuel allowance for engine start, taxi, takeoff, climb and 45 minutes reserve.*

75% Power at 8000 Ft	Range	820 nm
88 Gallons Usable Fuel	Time	5.9 hrs
Maximum Range at 10,000 Ft	Range	1025 nm
88 Gallons Usable Fuel	Time	9.6 hrs

RATE OF CLIMB AT SEA LEVEL — 865 fpm

SERVICE CEILING — 14,900 ft

TAKEOFF PERFORMANCE:

Ground Roll	805 ft
Total Distance Over 50-Ft Obstacle	1515 ft

LANDING PERFORMANCE:

Ground Roll	590 ft
Total Distance Over 50-Ft Obstacle	1350 ft

STALL SPEED (KCAS):

Flaps Up, Power Off	54 knots
Flaps Down, Power Off	49 knots

MAXIMUM WEIGHT:

Ramp	3110 lbs
Takeoff	3100 lbs
Landing	2950 lbs

STANDARD EMPTY WEIGHT — 1733 lbs

MAXIMUM USEFUL LOAD — 1377 lbs

BAGGAGE ALLOWANCE — 200 lbs

WING LOADING: *Pounds/Sq Ft* — 17.8

POWER LOADING: *Pounds/HP* — 13.5

FUEL CAPACITY: *Total* — 92 gal

OIL CAPACITY — 13 qts

ENGINE: *Teledyne Continental 230 BHP at 2400 RPM* — O-470-U

PROPELLER: *Constant Speed, Diameter* — 82 in

Table 8-2. 1970 Super Skylane performance & specifications.

GROSS WEIGHT	3600 lbs, 1633 kg
SPEED: *Best Power Mixture*	
Top Speed at Sea Level	174 mph, 280 kph
Cruise, 75% Power at 6000 Ft	163 mph, 262 kph
RANGE: *Normal Lean Mixture*	
Cruise, 75% Power at 6000 Ft	650 miles, 1045 km
63 Gallons, No Reserve	4.0 hours
	162 mph, 261 kph
Cruise, 75% Power at 6000 Ft	830 miles, 1335 km
80 Usable Gallons, No Reserve	5.1 hours
	162 mph, 261 kph
Optimum Range at 10,000 Ft	1020 miles, 1640 km
80 Usable Gallons, No Reserve	7.6 hours
	134 mph, 216 kph
RATE OF CLIMB AT SEA LEVEL	920 fpm, 280 mpm
SERVICE CEILING	14,800 ft, 4511 m
TAKEOFF:	
Ground Run	910 ft, 277 m
Total Distance Over 50-Ft Obstacle	1810 ft, 552 m
LANDING:	
Ground Roll	735 ft, 224 m
Total Distance Over 50-Ft Obstacle	1395 ft, 425 m
STALL SPEED:	
Flaps Up, Power Off	70 mph, 113 kph
Flaps Down, Power Off	61 mph, 98 kph
EMPTY WEIGHT: *(Approx.)*	1835 lbs, 832 kg
USEFUL LOAD	1765 lbs, 801 kg
WING LOADING	20.7 lbs/sq ft, 100.8 kg/sq. m
POWER LOADING	12.6 lbs/hp, 5.7 kg/hp
FUEL CAPACITY: *Total*	
Standard Tanks	65 gallons, 246 liters
Optional Long-Range Tanks	84 gallons, 318 liters
OIL CAPACITY: *Total*	12 quarts, 11.4 liters
POWER	Six-Cylinder, Fuel-Injection Engine, 285 Rated hp at 2700 rpm
PROPELLER:	
Two-Bladed, Constant-Speed—Diameter	82 inches, 2.08 m
WING AREA	174 sq ft, 16.2 sq m
LENGTH	28 ft 3 in, 8.61 m
HEIGHT: *(With Depressed Nose Strut)*	9 ft 7½ in, 2.93 m

Performance with optional three-bladed propeller is essentially the same as above.

Table 8-3. 1970 Turbo Super Skylane performance & specifications.

GROSS WEIGHT	3600 lbs, 1633 kg
SPEED: *Best Power Mixture*	
Top Speed at 19,000 Ft	200 mph, 322 kph
Cruise, 75% Power at 24,000 Ft	184 mph, 296 kph
Cruise, 75% Power at 10,000 Ft	170 mph, 274 kph
RANGE: *Normal Lean Mixture*	
Cruise, 75% Power at 24,000 Ft	700 miles, 1127 km
63 Usable Gallons, No Reserve	3.8 hours
	182 mph, 293 kph
Cruise, 75% Power at 10,000 Ft	645 miles, 1038 km
63 Usable Gallons, No Reserve	3.8 hours
	168 mph, 270 kph
Cruise, 75% Power at 24,000 Ft	890 miles, 1432 km
80 Usable Gallons, No Reserve	4.9 hours
	182 mph, 293 kph
Cruise, 75% Power at 10,000 Ft	820 miles, 1320 km
80 Usable Gallons, No Reserve	4.9 hours
	168 mph, 270 kph
Optimum Range at 15,000 Ft	1050 miles, 1690 km
80 Usable Gallons, No Reserve	7.6 hours
	139 mph, 224 kph
RATE OF CLIMB AT SEA LEVEL	1030 fpm, 314 mpm
SERVICE CEILING	26,300 ft, 8020 m
TAKEOFF:	
Ground Run	910 ft, 277 m
Total Distance Over 50-Ft Obstacle	1810 ft, 552 m
LANDING:	
Ground Roll	735 ft, 224 m
Total Distance Over 50-Ft Obstacle	1395 ft, 425 m
STALL SPEED:	
Flaps Up, Power Off	70 mph, 113 kph
Flaps Down, Power Off	61 mph, 98 kph
EMPTY WEIGHT: *(Approx.)*	1935 lbs, 878 kg
USEFUL LOAD	1665 lbs, 755 kg
WING LOADING	20.7 lbs/sq ft, 100.8 kg/sq m
POWER LOADING	12.6 lbs/hp, 5.7 kg/hp
FUEL CAPACITY: *Total*	
Standard Tanks	65 gallons, 246 liters
Optional Long-Range Tanks	84 gallons, 318 liters
OIL CAPACITY: *Total*	13 quarts, 12.3 liters
POWER	Six-Cylinder, Turbosupercharged, Fuel-Injection Engine, 285 Rated hp at 2700 rpm

Table 8-3. Continued.

PROPELLER:

Two-Bladed, Constant Speed—Diameter	82 inches, 2.08 m
WING SPAN	35 ft 10 in, 10.92 m
WING AREA	174 sq ft, 16.2 sq m
LENGTH	28 ft 3 in, 8.61 m
HEIGHT: *(With Depressed Nose Strut)*	9 ft 7½ in, 2.93 m

Performance with optional three-bladed propeller is essentially the same as above.

9

Cessna 206 and 207

THE FIRST CESSNA 206 was the 1965 model, first called the "Super Skywagon." It was directly descended from the Model 205 which had been produced 1962–64 inclusive. The 206 was built around the same basic airframe as the 205, though the fuselage was beefed-up to permit heavy floor loads and allow a 3½-ft double cargo door. It used the Model 210D Centurion wing (introduced on the 1964 Model 210) with 18.9 feet of flap and Frise type ailerons of increased chord. Its tail group was a slightly-modified version of the 210 empennage.

In 1966, the Turbo Super Skywagon was added to Cessna's "Utiline" series making a total of four single-engine utility craft. These were the Models 180, 185 Skywagon, Super Skywagon, and Turbo Super Skywagon. These latter two aircraft became, respectively, the Skywagon 206 and the Turbo Skywagon 206 in 1970 because the Model 207 was in the market by then and it would have had to be, presumably, the "Super Duper Skywagon" had the smaller craft kept the name "Super Skywagon."

TENACIOUS TERMINOLOGY

If you find all this confusing . . . Cessna's often ill-invented and not-necessarily-descriptive terms also include many component parts of Cessna airplanes. We say, "unfortunately" because we think this cheapens a good product. A "Utiline" fitted with a "Quick-Scan" panel of "Space Age gray" featuring "Accru-Measure" fuel gauges, sounds like something dreamed up in Detroit rather than in Wichita. And we'll apologize to Cessna for voicing this pet peeve just as soon as we hear a Cessna owner refer to his "Broad Span" elevators or his "Sure-Grip" control knobs as such.

The Skywagon 206 was discontinued in 1971 after 1,578 had been built. The last ones were priced at $25,995 and $30,495, the latter being the Turbo version.

STATIONAIR

The Cessna Stationair was introduced in 1971, obviously replacing the 206 Skywagon—or perhaps, more accurately, a simple renaming of the 206. In any case,

1967 P206B

the two are essentially the same airplane. Same airframe; same engine; new detail pretties, and a $3,000 price increase.

For 1972, the Stationair received the new Cessna wing with a slightly modified airfoil for improved slow flight handling, and a new nose cap containing the landing and taxi lights. After that, there were only detail changes through the 1976 model, by which time prices were up to $41,850 for the standard Stationair; $47,850 for the Turbo Stationair, and ranging upward to $52,150 for the Stationair II with complete avionics, and $58,200 for the Turbo Stationair II similarly equipped.

In 1978, it came equipped with a 28-volt electrical system and optional club seating. There were no further changes until Cessna stopped single-engine aircraft production in 1986. The 1986 price of a Stationair 6 was $111,400. This aircraft, in average condition, has a value of about $150,000 in 1992. Available modifications for the 206 include an engine/propeller upgrade offered by Carter Power, plus the usual wingtips and long-range tanks. Only a few ADs are on the 206. Like the 180 and 182, some models have the fuel cell problem and require quick drains and a 12-month inspection. The rear wing spar also needs inspection and/or strengthening, and there is an inspection note on the IO-520 engine.

SKYWAGON

The Cessna Skywagon 207, introduced in 1969, is the real minibus of the industry. With a 14-ft cabin, the 207 provides 156 cubic feet inside, which comfortably hauls seven any-sized adults and, apparently, all their worldly goods. In addition to luggage space in the aft cabin and a 300-lb-capacity optional cargo pod slung beneath the fuselage, the 207 also has a 120-lb capacity forward luggage compartment in its stretched nose between the firewall and cabin. And because this working airplane has an economical cruise that consumes as little as 10 gallons of fuel per hour, any air taxi operator that doesn't make money with it, just ain't tryin'.

1978 Stationair 6

Actually, this might be slightly overstating the case for the 207. It has a useful load of 1,920 lbs, which is 40 lbs more than its empty dry weight, but this is without seats, avionics, and fuel. Full tanks and all necessary equipment will leave about 1,400 lbs for people and baggage; but even that transposes into seven 170-pounders and 200 lbs of luggage. The loading limits of this craft are such that one may distribute this (approximate) 1,400 lbs pretty much as he pleases, although the plane does fly better with some load well aft.

Both 207 Models have the tubular-steel gear legs and the resulting luxurious taxi.

TURBO SKYWAGON

The Turbo Skywagon 207 can operate easily from high altitude airports and can handle nonstandard days with an extra margin of safety. At its 3,800-lb gross weight, it climbs 885 fpm at sea level and has a 24,500-ft service ceiling. The Turbo 207 can reach a top speed of 189 mph and a cruise speed of 176 mph at 75 percent power at 20,000 feet. Range is 725 miles (with reserve fuel remaining) at 20,000 and 75 percent.

Our evaluation of the Turbo 207 came on a damp and overcast November day when we were joined by two newspaper reporters and three others, plus the Cessna pilot, for a purely local flight.

Because the turbo system best reveals its muscle on hot days and/or in the high places, this wasn't a very good demonstration of the difference it makes; however, we did have seven people aboard, and with a good deal of optional equipment installed and about 50 gallons of fuel, we were within 150–175 lbs of the plane's maximum allowable weight. Ground temperature was 39 degrees F, wind was 3–5 mph down the runway, and airport elevation 1,108 ft.

Engine-start procedure is simple. With electrical switches off and cowl flaps open, turn on the master switch and set parking brake. Then, mixture "Full Rich,"prop in "High rpms"; with throttle closed, punch the "Lo" side of the auxil-

1978 Stationair 7

iary fuel pump switch, turn ignition key to "Start," and slowly advance the throttle. With the engine idling satisfactorily, turn off the aux fuel pump (which acts as an automatic primer when cranking the engine), turn on radios and electrics.

The auxiliary fuel pump, which comes with fuel-injected engines, plus the constant-speed prop, cowl flaps and rudder trim, are the new controls to get used to if you're transitioning from the smaller or older Cessnas.

With the 13-item pretakeoff check completed, our demo pilot dropped 10 degrees of flap and applied full power. He came back on the control column as we reached 70 mph and we were airborne. Seconds later, the rate-of-climb needle settled on 900 fpm as our pilot cut back to 75 percent power and adjusted the climb with the wheel at a shade under 100 mph IAS. He leaned the mixture slightly as we climbed, but nothing else changed—except a slowly-increasing airspeed—and we were still showing 900 fpm, at 100 mph, when we leveled off at 5,000. This of course represented a gain in TAS, with no loss in climb rate, at that altitude.

TRUE AIRSPEED 160 MPH

Our density altitude was a bit lower than that showing on the altimeter, and in cruise, TAS worked out to 160 mph turning 2,500 rpms with 25 inches of manifold pressure, while the fuel flow meter registered 16 gallons per hour fuel consumption.

We weren't shown any stalls, because three of our passengers were new to "little" airplanes and our pilot wisely wanted to give them a smooth, confidence-building ride. He told us that 207 stalls are sedate, almost leisurely, and contain no surprises. Because we were impressed with his deliberate and conservative handling of the airplane, we decided his assessment would be accurate.

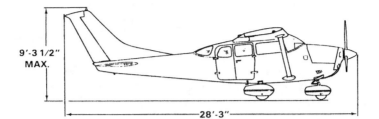

9'-3 1/2"
MAX.

28'-3"

NOTES:
1. Dimensions shown are based on standard empty weight and proper nose gear and tire inflation.

2. Dimensions shown reflect standard nose and main gear tire installation.

3. Wing span shown with strobe lights installed.

4. Maximum height shown with nose gear depressed as far as possible.

5. Wheel base length is 69 1/4".

6. Propeller ground clearance is 11 3/4".

7. Wing area is 174 square feet.

8. Minimum turning radius (✳ pivot point to outboard wing tip) is 26'-3".

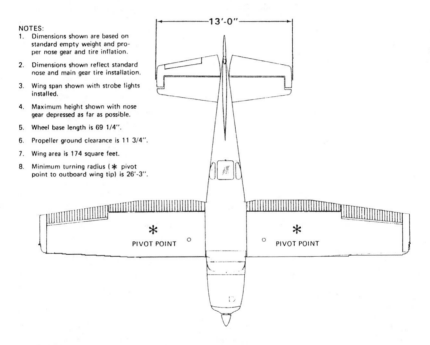

13'-0"

✳
PIVOT POINT

✳
PIVOT POINT

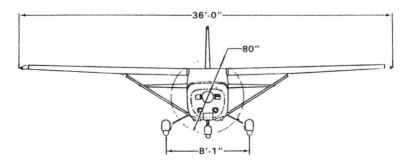

36'-0"

80"

8'-1"

1986 Stationair 6 (U206G) views

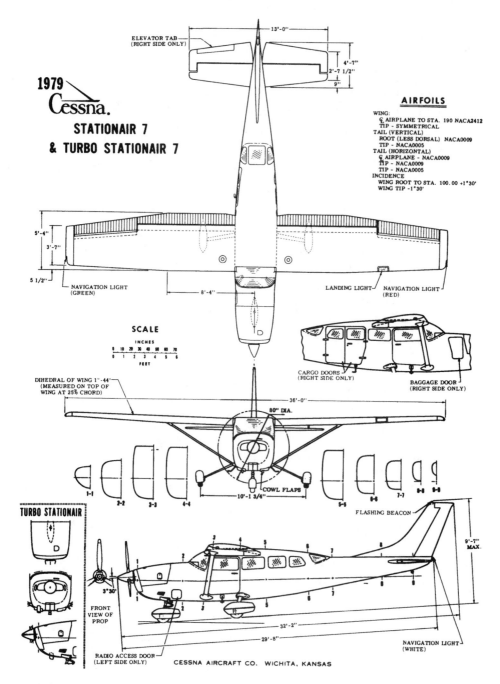

ELEVATOR TAB
(RIGHT SIDE ONLY)

13'-0"

4'-7"
2'-7 1/2"
9"

1979
Cessna.

STATIONAIR 7
& TURBO STATIONAIR 7

AIRFOILS

WING:
₵ AIRPLANE TO STA. 190 NACA2412
TIP - SYMMETRICAL
TAIL (VERTICAL)
ROOT (LESS DORSAL) NACA0009
TIP - NACA0005
TAIL (HORIZONTAL)
₵ AIRPLANE - NACA0009
TIP - NACA0009
TIP - NACA0005
INCIDENCE
WING ROOT TO STA. 100.00 +1°30'
WING TIP -1°30'

5'-4"
3'-7"

5 1/2"

NAVIGATION LIGHT
(GREEN)

8'-4"

LANDING LIGHT   NAVIGATION LIGHT
(RED)

CARGO DOORS
(RIGHT SIDE ONLY)

BAGGAGE DOOR
(RIGHT SIDE ONLY)

SCALE

INCHES
0 10 20 30 40 50 60 70
0   1   2   3   4   5   6
FEET

DIHEDRAL OF WING 1"-44'
(MEASURED ON TOP OF
WING AT 25% CHORD)

36'-0"

80" DIA.

1-1
2-2   3-3   4-4

COWL FLAPS

10'-1 3/4"

5-5

6-6   7-7

8-8 9-9

FLASHING BEACON

9'-7"
MAX.

TURBO STATIONAIR

FRONT
VIEW OF
PROP

3°30'

RADIO ACCESS DOOR
(LEFT SIDE ONLY)

32'-2"

29'-8"

NAVIGATION LIGHT
(WHITE)

CESSNA AIRCRAFT CO. WICHITA, KANSAS

1979 Stationair 7 views

He showed us two "grease job" landings and he sure made landing look easy. His approach was at 95 mph, slowing to 85 mph on final with full flaps. Then an unhurried, graceful flare, with throttle closed, brought touchdown on the main wheels at 65 mph. Rollout required about 500 feet.

Cessna's improvements to the airplane included various aesthetic changes and a 28-volt electrical system up to 1975; in 1977, a 3-blade propeller and a TSIO-520-M engine was offered. In 1978, the 207 series was renamed the Stationair 7 and Turbo Stationair 7, which lasted until 1984. In 1980, the Stationair 8 series was added as an 8-seat version. The final years for these models are 1977 for the Stationair 206, 1986 for the Stationair 6, 1977 for the Skywagon 207, 1979 for the Stationair 7, and 1984 for the Stationair 8. Modifications of the 207 include STOL conversion kits and long-range tanks. The ADs are much the same as for the 206.

Some sample prices: 1985 Stationair 6, $104,100 compared to 1992 used for $137,000; 1983 Stationair 8, $126,300, compared to 1992 used for $128,000; 1978 Stationair 7, $63,200, compared to 1992 used for $72,000.

Table 9-1. 1979 Stationair 7 performance & specifications.

SPEED:

Maximum at Sea Level	150 knots	278 kph
Cruise, 75% Power at 6500 feet	143 knots	265 kph

CRUISE: Recommended lean mixture with fuel
allowance for engine start, taxi, takeoff,
climb and 45 minutes reserve at 45% power

75% Power at 6500 Ft with	390 nm	722 km
54 Gallons Usable Fuel	2.8 hr	2.8 hr
75% Power at 6500 Ft with	565 nm	1046 km
73 Gallons Usable Fuel	4.0 hr	4.0 hr
Maximum Range at 10,000 Ft with	470 nm	870 km
54 Gallons Usable Fuel	4.2 hr	4.2 hr
Maximum Range at 10,000 Ft with	690 nm	1278 km
73 Gallons Usable Fuel	6.2 hr	6.2 hr

RATE OF CLIMB AT SEA LEVEL	810 fpm	247 mpm
SERVICE CEILING	13,300 ft	4054 m

TAKEOFF PERFORMANCE:

Ground Roll	1100 ft	335 m
Total Distance Over 50-Ft Obstacle	1970 ft	600 m

LANDING PERFORMANCE:

Ground Roll	765 ft	233 m
Total Distance Over 50-Ft Obstacle	1500 ft	457 m

STALL SPEED (CAS):

Flaps Up, Power Off	65 knots	120 kph
Flaps Down, Power Off	58 knots	107 kph

MAXIMUM WEIGHT:

Ramp	3812 lb	1729 kg
Takeoff and Landing	3800 lb	1724 kg

STANDARD EMPTY WEIGHT:

Stationair 7	2076 lb	942 kg
Stationair 7 II	2145 lb	973 kg
Utility Stationair 7—1 Seat	1971 lb	894 kg
Utility Stationair 7 II—1 Seat	2040 lb	925 kg

MAXIMUM USEFUL LOAD:

Stationair 7	1736 lb	787 kg
Stationair 7 II	1667 lb	756 kg
Utility Stationair 7—1 Seat	1841 lb	835 kg
Utility Stationair 7 II—1 Seat	1772 lb	804 kg

BAGGAGE ALLOWANCE:	300 lb	136 kg
WING LOADING	21.8 lb/sq ft	107 kg/sq m
POWER LOADING	12.7 lb/hp	5.7 kg/hp
WING SPAN	35 ft, 10 in	10.92 m
WING AREA	174 sq ft	16.2 sq m
LENGTH	32 ft, 2 in	9.80 m
HEIGHT	9 ft, 7 in	2.92 m

FUEL CAPACITY, *Total:*

Standard Tanks	61 gal	231 liters
Long Range Tanks	80 gal	303 liters

OIL CAPACITY   12 qt   11.4 liters

ENGINE: *Teledyne Continental IO-520-F*
Injection Engine:

300 BHP at 2850 RPM (takeoff)
285 BHP at 2700 RPM (maximum continuous)

PROPELLER: *Constant Speed, 3 Blades,*
80 Inch Diameter (2.03 m)

NOTE: *Weight of Optional Nav-Pac Is:*   16 lb   7 kg

Table 9-2. 1979 Turbo Stationair 7 performance & specifications.

SPEED:

Maximum at 17,000 Ft	170 knots	315 kph
Cruise, 80% Power at 20,000 Ft	161 knots	298 kph
Cruise, 80% Power at 10,000 Ft	148 knots	274 kph

CRUISE: Recommended lean mixture with fuel
allowance for engine start, taxi, takeoff, climb
and 45 minutes reserve at 45% power

80% Power at 20,000 Ft with	350 nm	648 km
54 Gallons Usable Fuel	2.4 hr	2.4 hr
80% Power at 10,000 Ft with	345 nm	639 km
54 Gallons Usable Fuel	2.4 hr	2.4 hr
80% Power at 20,000 Ft with	525 nm	972 km
73 Gallons Usable Fuel	3.5 hr	3.5 hr
80% Power at 10,000 Ft with	510 nm	945 km
73 Gallons Usable Fuel	3.5 hr	3.5 hr
Maximum Range at 20,000 Ft with	385 nm	713 km
54 Gallons Usable Fuel	3.3 hr	3.3 hr
Maximum Range at 10,000 Ft with	415 nm	769 km
54 Gallons Usable Fuel	3.6 hr	3.6 hr
Maximum Range at 20,000 Ft with	585 nm	1083 km
73 Gallons Usable Fuel	5.0 hr	5.0 hr
Maximum Range at 10,000 Ft with	610 nm	1130 km
73 Gallons Usable Fuel	5.3 hr	5.3 hr

RATE OF CLIMB AT SEA LEVEL	885 fpm	270 mpm
SERVICE CEILING	26,000 ft	7925 m

TAKEOFF PERFORMANCE:

Ground Roll	1030 ft	314 m
Total Distance Over 50-Ft Obstacle	1860 ft	567 m

LANDING PERFORMANCE:

Ground Roll	765 ft	233 m
Total Distance Over 50-Ft Obstacle	1500 ft	457 m

STALL SPEED, (CAS):

Flaps Up, Power Off	65 knots	120 kph
Flaps Down, Power Off	58 knots	107 kph

MAXIMUM WEIGHT:

Ramp	3816 lb	1731 kg
Takeoff or Landing	3800 lb	1764 kg

STANDARD EMPTY WEIGHT:

Turbo Stationair 7	2157 lb	978 kg
Turbo Stationair 7 II	2226 lb	1010 kg
Utility Turbo Stationair 7—1 Seat	2052 lb	931 kg
Utility Turbo Stationair 7 II—1 Seat	2121 lb	962 kg

MAXIMUM USEFUL LOAD:

Turbo Stationair 7	1659 lb	753 kg
Turbo Stationair 7 II	1590 lb	721 kg
Utility Turbo Stationair 7—1 Seat	1764 lb	800 kg
Utility Turbo Stationair 7 II—1 Seat	1659 lb	769 kg

BAGGAGE ALLOWANCE	300 lb	136 kg
WING LOADING	21.8 lb/sq ft	107 kg/sq m
POWER LOADING	12.3 lb/hp	5.6 kg/hp
WING SPAN	35 ft, 10 in	10.92 m
WING AREA	174 sq ft	16.2 sq m
LENGTH	32 ft, 2 in	9.80 m
HEIGHT	9 ft, 7 in	2.92 m
FUEL CAPACITY, *Total:*		
Standard Tanks	61 gal	231 liters
Long Range Tanks	80 gal	303 liters
OIL CAPACITY	13 qt	12.3 liters

ENGINE: *Teledyne Continental TSIO-520-M*
    Turbocharged, Fuel Injection Engine:

310 BHP at 2700 RPM (takeoff)
285 BHP at 2600 RPM (maximum continuous)

PROPELLER: *Constant speed, 3 blades,*
    80 inch diameter (2.03 m)

NOTE: *Weight of optional Nav-Pac is:*   16 lb   7 kg

Table 9-3. 1986 Stationair 6 performance & specifications.

SPEED:

Maximum at Sea Level		156 knots
Cruise, 75% Power at 6500 Ft		147 knots

CRUISE: Recommended lean mixture with fuel allowance for engine start, taxi, takeoff, climb and 45 minutes reserve.

75% Power at 6500 Ft	Range	680 nm
88 Gallons Usable Fuel	Time	4.7 hrs
Maximum Range at 10,000 Ft	Range	900 nm
88 Gallons Usable Fuel	Time	7.7 hrs

RATE OF CLIMB AT SEA LEVEL 920 fpm

SERVICE CEILING 14,800 ft

TAKEOFF PERFORMANCE:

Ground Roll	900 ft
Total Distance Over 50-Ft Obstacle	1780 ft

LANDING PERFORMANCE:

Ground Roll	735 ft
Total Distance Over 50-Ft Obstacle	1395 ft

STALL SPEED (KCAS):

Flaps Up, Power Off	62 knots
Flaps Down, Power Off	54 knots

MAXIMUM WEIGHT:

Ramp	3612 lbs
Takeoff or Landing	3600 lbs

STANDARD EMPTY WEIGHT:

Stationalr 6	1946 lbs
Utility Stationair 6	1919 lbs

MAXIMUM USEFUL LOAD:

Stationair 6	1666 lbs
Utility Stationair 6	1693 lbs

BAGGAGE ALLOWANCE 180 lbs

WING LOADING: Pounds/Sq Ft 20.7

POWER LOADING: Pounds/HP 12.0

FUEL CAPACITY: Total 92 gal

OIL CAPACITY 13 qts

ENGINE: Teledyne Continental, Fuel Injection   IO-520-F
300 BHP at 2850 RPM (5-Minute Takeoff Rating)
285 BHP at 2700 RPM (Maximum Continuous Rating)

PROPELLER: 3-Bladed, Constant Speed, Diameter   80 in

10

Cessna 210

THE FIRST CESSNA 210 was the 1960 Model, announced late in 1959. At that time, many of us tended to think of it as a slicked-up 182 with a crazy retract gear and bigger engine (IO-470E fuel-injected Continental of 260-hp), but it wasn't. It was an all-new design aimed at the Bonanza/Comanche market. It had a top speed of 199 mph, a cruise (75% @ 7,000) of 190 mph and should have been right on target; but customer acceptance was slow. Ten years later, sales of this craft still lagged behind Cessna's expectations and the explanation remained obscure, probably clouded by an unvoiced (and unreasoned) customer prejudice—perhaps something some people didn't like about the plane and were ashamed or reluctant to admit.

We're guessing about this because we don't know why Cessna's top performer in the single-engine class has not taken a bigger share of that market. From the beginning, it has performed just as Cessna claimed, and has never been accused of possessing any vicious traits.

Anyway, beginning with the 1969 Model, the question—if it remains—will have to come from the other side of our mouth, because the new Centurions (new 210) are different airplanes and demand fresh evaluations.

CENTURION

Known as the "210" during its first four years of production, this design became the "Centurion" in 1964 when it received a redesigned wing with more flap area, four additional inches on the tail surfaces and the IO-520A 285-hp engine (turtle deck with back windows was added in 1962, along with four extra inches of cabin width). In 1967, the Centurion appeared with a full-cantilever wing; and in 1968 deicing and anti-icing systems for prop, wing, and tail were offered.

But the strutless Centurions of 1967–68, though structurally sound, apparently didn't look that way to many because of their pronounced (three degrees) dihedral. At least that was Cessna's conclusion. Therefore, the cantilever wing was flattened-out on the 1969 Model, with only one degree of dihedral remaining, and the ailerons interconnected with the rudder via a spring load to keep good stability.

1978 Centurion

Then, in 1970, the Centurion received a 25 percent bigger cabin to make it a full six-place airplane, with new side windows extending sans posts almost half the length of the cabin. Also in 1970, the Centurion went to the tubular-steel main-gear legs for softer landings and a wider stance (the nosewheel strut was shortened on the 1969 Model, and the "chin" housing eliminated).

The new gear retracts completely into the fuselage within a few seconds at the touch of a control on the pedestal. The system has a fluid reservoir and is under pressure only during the time the gear is being activated. This improves reliability and should reduce service costs.

The cabin is accessible through a yard-wide door on each side, and offers a full assortment of convenience items such as individual air vents, ash trays, cigarette lighter, and magazine pockets—all close at hand. Other standard cabin accessories include sun visors, map pockets, arm rests, an integrally-mounted overhead light console for the pilot's area and individual lights above the passenger seats.

Some of the purists might complain about the inter-connected roll and yaw controls, but this objection won't be as "pure" as the gung-ho crowd will have you believe because this principle was employed by the Wright brothers on the world's first successful airplane. It seems to us that the only pilots who have a valid objection to interconnected controls are the aerobatic types; Cessna clearly didn't intend that anyone should slow-roll the Centurion across country at 200 miles per; however, you can override the spring-load interconnect anytime you want or need to.

TRANSITIONING

If you've been flying a Super Skylane or anything of comparable muscle, transition to the Centurion will be easy. But if you're accustomed to smaller and slower craft, you really should have at least three hours of dual (and a minimum of 150

1978 Pressurized Centurion

hours in your logbook) before sashaying off to far away places in this—or any other—high performance retractable. It is a big airplane, and a sudden one. Cruising at 185–190 mph requires that you think more than one checkpoint ahead in matters of fuel management, efficient letdowns and weather evaluation. In short, it's a lot more airplane than a Skyhawk, and it demands a higher level of competence to safely operate it. [Editor's note: Since this was written, insurance requirements have placed more demands on pilot experience and ratings when a pilot is considering obtaining an airplane. Those insurance requirements of today might have a greater impact on any purchasing decision than in the past.]

We don't mean by this that the Centurion is physically hard to fly. It is not. It is very stable, with a solid, big-airplane feel, as a long-legged personal transport should be. What we mean by "higher level of competence" is that, as aircraft weight and speed goes up, so does the penalty for error.

TURBO CENTURION

The Turbo Centurion is of course the high-altitude performer, and the one that makes a "standard day" out of a hot and humid one. The turbo system assures maximum horsepower up to 19,000 feet, and beyond that keeps working to compress the thin air into a richer source of oxygen for the engine. This system adds no extra controls to adjust or gauges to monitor, and no constant adjusting of the throttle is required during the climb to 19,000. The turbine is automatically regulated by an absolute pressure controller and an over-boost control valve that automatically bleeds off excessive compressor discharge pressure. And all this is housed in a—wouldn't you just know it?—"Jet-Flow" cowling.

The Turbo Centurion comes with a 74-cubic-foot capacity oxygen system as standard equipment. This system includes an overhead oxygen console with a capacity gauge system control, control wheel microphone switch, and automatic regulator.

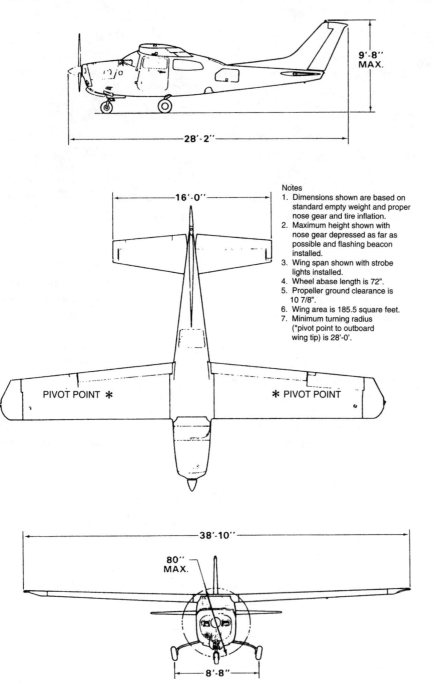

Notes
1. Dimensions shown are based on standard empty weight and proper nose gear and tire inflation.
2. Maximum height shown with nose gear depressed as far as possible and flashing beacon installed.
3. Wing span shown with strobe lights installed.
4. Wheel abase length is 72".
5. Propeller ground clearance is 10 7/8".
6. Wing area is 185.5 square feet.
7. Minimum turning radius (*pivot point to outboard wing tip) is 28'-0'.

PIVOT POINT ✱

✱ PIVOT POINT

1986 Centurion (210R)

After introduction of the Turbo Centurion, modifications in 1980 included a range of refinements including a higher flap-down speed, standby generator, de-icing equipment, weather radar, and other options. In 1985, the cowling was re-designed, gear-down speed was increased to 165 knots, and some cosmetics were added. The gross weight was increased from 4,000 pounds in 1984 to 4,100 for the 1985 model. In 1985, a new 325 hp TSIO-520-CE engine was made available for both fixed and retractable gear models. The final production year was 1986.

POPULAR MODIFICATIONS

The Centurion has proven popular with the modification groups. In addition to STOL kits, long-range tanks, baggage compartment fuel, and other such modifications, there is a control surface improvement for rudder, elevator, and ailerons offered by O & N Aircraft Modifications.

As a popular high-performance aircraft, the 210 has a good share of ADs that you need to watch out for. Among these are the usual seat rail item, the fuel cell item (inspect every 12 months, install a quick drain), several engine items, and selection of 1,000-hour landing gear inspection ADs.

The 1985 list prices were $133,950 for a retractable Centurion and $154,900 for a Turbo Centurion. Current used prices for these models are $170,000 and $186,000, respectively.

Table 10-1. Centurion (210R) performance & specifications.

SPEED:

Maximum at Sea Level	175 knots
Cruise, 75% Power at 7000 Ft	169 knots

CRUISE: Recommended lean mixture with fuel allowance for engine start, taxi, takeoff, climb and 45 minutes reserve.

75% Power at 7000 Ft	770 nm
522 Pounds Usable Fuel	4.6 hrs
75% Power at 7000 Ft	1070 nm
690 Pounds Usable Fuel	4.6 hrs
Maximum Range at 10,000 Ft	1010 nm
522 Pounds Usable Fuel	7.7 hrs
Maximum Range at 10,000 Ft	1390 nm
690 Pounds Usable Fuel	10.6 hrs

RATE OF CLIMB AT SEA LEVEL	1060 fpm
SERVICE CEILING	16,000 ft

TAKEOFF PERFORMANCE:

Ground Roll	1215 ft
Total Distance Over 50-Ft Obstacle	2050 ft

LANDING PERFORMANCE:

Ground Roll	815 ft
Total Distance Over 50-Ft Obstacle	1585 ft

STALL SPEED (KCAS):

Flaps Up, Power Off	63 knots
Flaps Down, Power Off	53 knots

MAXIMUM WEIGHT:

Ramp	3862 lbs
Takeoff or Landing	3850 lbs

STANDARD EMPTY WEIGHT	2220 lbs
MAXIMUM USEFUL LOAD	1642 lbs
BAGGAGE ALLOWANCE: Maximum With 4 People	240 lbs
WING LOADING: Pounds/Sq Ft	20.8
POWER LOADING: Pounds/HP	12.8

FUEL CAPACITY:

Standard Tanks	90 gal
Long Range Tanks	120 gal

OIL CAPACITY	11 qts
ENGINE: Teledyne Continental, Fuel Injection	IO-520-L

300 BHP at 2850 RPM (5-Minute Takeoff Rating)
285 BHP at 2700 RPM (Maximum Continuous Rating)

PROPELLER: 3-Bladed Constant Speed, Diameter	80 in

11

Cessna Cardinal RG

CESSNA'S ANSWER TO THE PIPER CHEROKEE ARROW 200 and Beechcraft Sierra was the Cardinal RG, with retractable landing gear, introduced in 1971. All use the same engine (different "dash numbers") and on paper, at least, specs and performance figures for all three are so close together they are almost interchangeable. Basic list price of the Cardinal RG in 1976, at $35,550, was $900 below basic list of the Sierra and about $2,000 above the Arrow's base price.

These three airplanes do handle differently. The Cardinal RG has the gentlest stall, mushing straight ahead with the wheel full back. The Sierra's ailerons are sharper, but soft ailerons have always been a Cessna trait. Cardinal RG pitch control is a bit heavier compared to both low-wingers; rudder seems about the same. Nothing to pick at on any of the three, really. So, in the end, it comes down to a matter of personal preferences. We like the Cardinal because its wing is on top. In hot weather and in rainy weather, that makes a big difference. And because the Cardinal RG's wing is positioned mainly behind the pilot, one doesn't give away all that much in upward visibility.

ATTENTION-GETTING

The Cardinal RG is deserving of special attention as the most popular and glamorous of Cessna's retractable gear models. While both the 172 and 182 have been offered in retractable gear models, the Cardinal version has gathered the most attention.

In 1972, the Cardinal RG received a redesigned propeller that added a little to its performance in both speed and rate-of-climb. In 1973, ten gallons were added to its fuel capacity for a total of 61 gallons; and the front seats were made vertically adjustable. The following year, the Cardinal RG was given a new cabin heating and ventilation system and in 1976, strengthened wheels and brakes, along with a redesigned instrument panel and a dozen minor detail improvements. In its last production year, 1978, it got the 28-volt electrical system.

In 1978, the final production year, the RG II was offered at $43,950; this plane was valued at about $40,000 on the 1992 used market.

1978 Cardinal RG

The Cardinal RG's market position was partially taken by the Cutlass RG, a "boosted" version of the 172 developed in 1979 and produced in 1980. Unfortunately, this model was introduced at a particularly rough time, and sold very few units. The 182 was also produced in an RG version in 1988. It was called the Skylane RG, and featured a gross weight of 3,100 pounds, and a 235 hp Lycoming engine. It lasted up to 1986. (The Cessna 182 chapter has more details about the Skylane RG.)

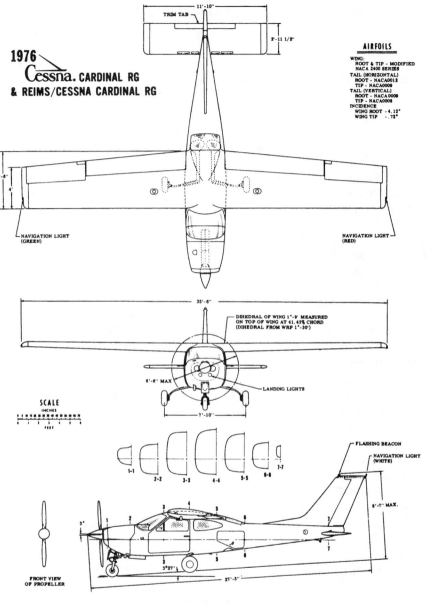

1976
Cessna. CARDINAL RG
& REIMS/CESSNA CARDINAL RG

11'-10"

TRIM TAB

2'-11 1/2"

5'-6"

4'

NAVIGATION LIGHT
(GREEN)

NAVIGATION LIGHT
(RED)

35'-6"

DIHEDRAL OF WING 1°-9' MEASURED
ON TOP OF WING AT 41.43% CHORD
(DIHEDRAL FROM WRP 1°-30')

6'-6" MAX.

LANDING LIGHTS

7'-10"

SCALE
INCHES

FEET

FLASHING BEACON

NAVIGATION LIGHT
(WHITE)

8'-7" MAX.

1-1
2-2
3-3
4-4
5-5
6-6
7-7

FRONT VIEW
OF PROPELLER

3°27'

27'-3"

CESSNA AIRCRCRAFT CO.   WICHITA, KANSAS

1976 Cardinal RG views

Table 11-1. Cardinal 177RG performance & specifications.

SPEED:

Maximum at Sea Level	156 knots	289 kph
Cruise, 75% Power at 7000 Ft	148 knots	274 kph

CRUISE: *Recommended Lean Mixture with fuel allowance
for engine start, taxi, takeoff, climb and 45 minutes
reserve at 45% power*

75% Power at 7000 Ft with *60 Gal Usable Fuel*	715 nm 4.9 hr	1324 km 4.9 hr
Maximum Range at 10,000 Ft with *60 Gal Usable Fuel*	895 nm 7.5 hr	1658 km 7.5 hr

RATE OF CLIMB AT SEA LEVEL	925 fpm	282 mpm
SERVICE CEILING	17,100 ft	5210 m

TAKEOFF PERFORMANCE:

Ground Roll	890 ft	271 m
Total Distance Over 50-Ft Obstacle	1585 ft	483 m

LANDING PERFORMANCE:

Ground Roll	730 ft	223 m
Total Distance Over 50-Ft Obstacle	1350 ft	411 m

STALL SPEED, (CAS):

Flaps Up, Power Off	57 knots	106 kph
Flaps Down, Power Off	50 knots	93 kph

MAXIMUM WEIGHT	2800 lb	1270 kg

STANDARD EMPTY WEIGHT:

Cardinal RG	1707 lb	774 kg
Cardinal RG II	1768 lb	802 kg

MAXIMUM USEFUL LOAD

Cardinal RG	1093 lb	496 kg
Cardinal RG II	1032 lb	468 kg

BAGGAGE ALLOWANCE	120 lb	54 kg
WING LOADING	16.1 lb/sq ft	78.6 kg/sq m
POWER LOADING	14.0 lb/hp	6.4 kg/hp
WING SPAN	35 ft, 6 in	10.82 m
WING AREA	174 sq ft	16.2 sq m
LENGTH	27 ft, 3 in	8.31 m
HEIGHT	8 ft, 7 in	2.62 m
FUEL CAPACITY, *Total:*	61 gal	231 liters
OIL CAPACITY	9 qt	8.5 liters

ENGINE: *Avco Lycoming IO-360-A1B6D Engine;
200 BHP at 2700 RPM*

PROPELLER: *Constant Speed, 2 blades,
78 Inch Diameter (1.98 m)*

12

Cessna ag aircraft

CESSNA ENTERED THE AGRICULTURAL AIRCRAFT FIELD in 1966 with its AGwagon and within five years dominated the market, offering the AGwagon with a choice of 230 or 300 hp. In 1972, three additional agcraft were added: the AGtruck, AGcarryall, and AGpickup. The 230-hp AGpickup was the economy model, and was discontinued in 1976.

All low-wing models featured the new "Camber-Lift" wing in 1972; and the high-wing AGcarryall was fitted with it in 1973. Translated, "Camber-Lift" means that Cessna aerodynamicists slightly reshaped the time-proven NACA 2412 airfoil to produce tighter turns and improved slow-flight characteristics without a penalty to other performance. It was a good move, despite the stupid name. Camber lift, indeed. Is there any other kind?

Cessna's AG-craft were so well conceived in the beginning that experience revealed nothing of significance that required modifying airframes or engines. Most of the improvements were in the aircraft's dispersal systems. The changes encompassed such things as new voltage regulator ('76), better cabin ventilation ('75), air intake on fin to pressurize tailcone and against chemicals infiltration ('75), new strut fairings ('73), and the like.

COMPETITIVE PRESSURES

In 1978, the 28-volt electrical system was made standard on all models. The Ag Husky appeared in 1979, offering a 310-hp turbo engine. From 1977 until 1983, when all Cessna agricultural production ceased, these models came under increasing competition from larger competitors in the agplane marketplace. With dwindling production and a sick economy, it was no longer possible to remain competitive.

Innovative and adaptive use of aerial application presents far-reaching possibilities for a worldwide increase in population of food and fiber products. Nowadays, double-cropping, accomplished by aerial seeding of a second crop into stands of existing ones, tends to extend the growing year and allow the farmer to get two crops from the same land. Fertilization, seeding, weed control, insect control, defoliation, and desiccation are established practices currently performed by

1978 Cessna AGtruck

air that contribute markedly to increased agricultural output. Chemical stimulation of growing crops, and range-fire control are new uses for agricultural aircraft that are now showing good results.

The AGwagon and AGtruck employ the same airframe and same 300-hp en-

1967 Ag Husky

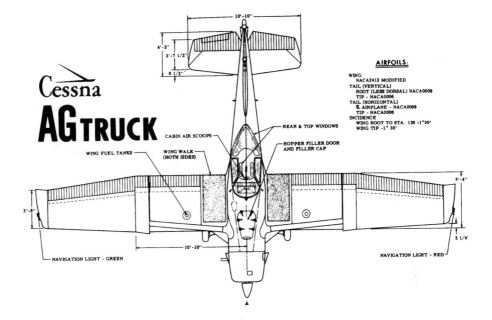

Cessna AGTRUCK

AIRFOILS:

WING:
NACA2412 MODIFIED
TAIL (VERTICAL)
ROOT (LESS DORSAL) NACA0009
TIP - NACA0006
TAIL (HORIZONTAL)
℄ AIRPLANE - NACA0009
TIP - NACA0006
INCIDENCE
WING ROOT TO STA. 129 +1°30'
WING TIP -1° 30'

REAR & TOP WINDOWS

CABIN AIR SCOOPS

HOPPER FILLER DOOR
AND FILLER CAP

WING FUEL TANKS

WING WALK
(BOTH SIDES)

10'-10"

4'-2"
2'-7 1/2"
6 1/2"

5'-4"

5 1/4"

3'-8"

10'-10"

NAVIGATION LIGHT - GREEN

NAVIGATION LIGHT - RED

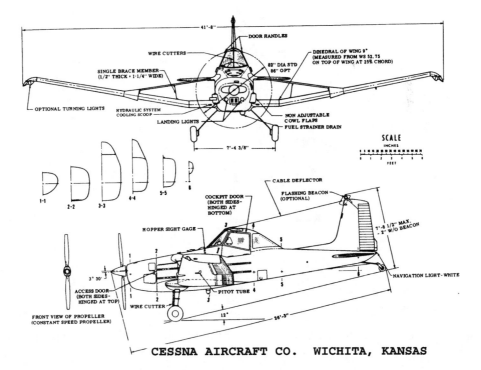

41'-8"

DOOR HANDLES

WIRE CUTTERS

DIHEDRAL OF WING 9°
(MEASURED FROM WS 52.75
ON TOP OF WING AT 25% CHORD)

SINGLE BRACE MEMBER
(1/2" THICK • 1-1/4" WIDE)

82" DIA STD
86" OPT

OPTIONAL TURNING LIGHTS

HYDRAULIC SYSTEM
COOLING SCOOP

LANDING LIGHTS

NON ADJUSTABLE
COWL FLAPS

FUEL STRAINER DRAIN

7'-4 3/8"

SCALE
INCHES
FEET

1-1
2-2
3-3
4-4
5-5

CABLE DEFLECTOR

FLASHING BEACON
(OPTIONAL)

COCKPIT DOOR
(BOTH SIDES-
HINGED AT
BOTTOM)

7'-8 1/2" MAX.
2" W/O BEACON

HOPPER SIGHT GAGE

NAVIGATION LIGHT- WHITE

ACCESS DOOR
(BOTH SIDES-
HINGED AT TOP)

PITOT TUBE

3° 30'

WIRE CUTTER

12"

26'-3"

FRONT VIEW OF PROPELLER
(CONSTANT SPEED PROPELLER)

CESSNA AIRCRAFT CO.   WICHITA, KANSAS

AG Truck views

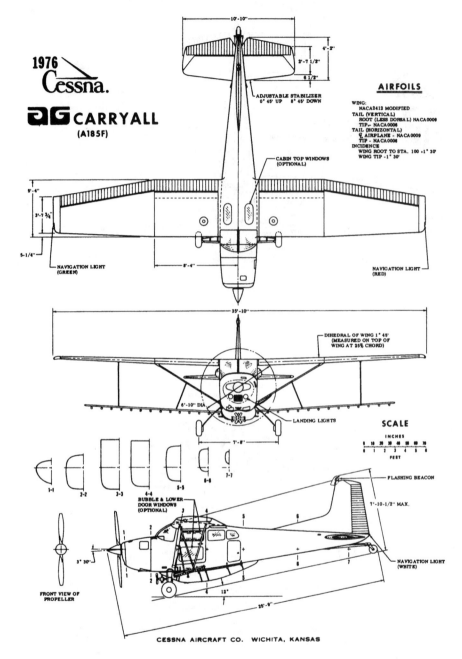

1976 AGcarryall views

gine with constant-speed propellers. The AGcarryall, with a hopper capacity of 151 gals (as opposed to 200 gals for the AGwagon, and 280 gals for the AGtruck), is designed as an all-purpose agplane. The AGcarryall comes equipped with a liquid dispersal system. Optional equipment includes seating for up to six adults.

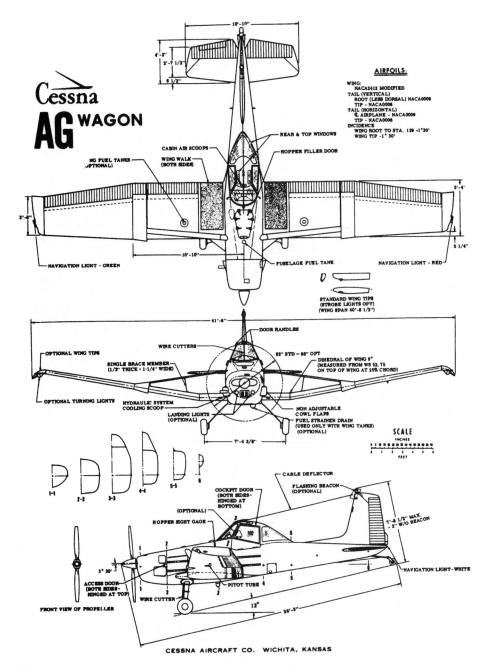

AGwagon views

STUDENT TRAINER

With its center-mounted dispersal controls, the AGcarryall is an excellent student trainer and general purpose craft for aerial application operators. It is a good

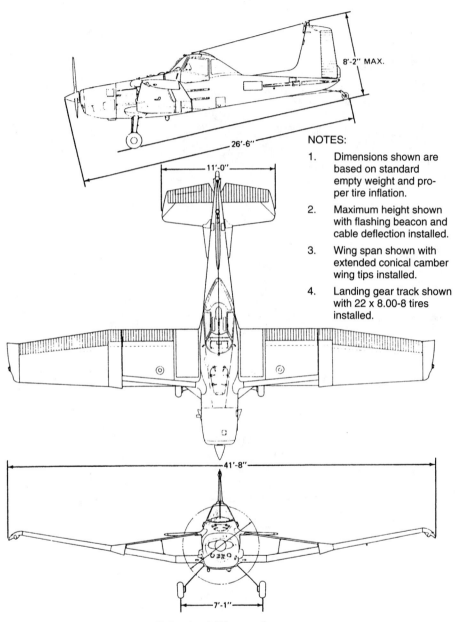

8'-2" MAX.

26'-6"

11'-0"

41'-8"

7'-1"

NOTES:

1. Dimensions shown are based on standard empty weight and proper tire inflation.

2. Maximum height shown with flashing beacon and cable deflection installed.

3. Wing span shown with extended conical camber wing tips installed.

4. Landing gear track shown with 22 x 8.00-8 tires installed.

Principal Dimensions

1979 Ag Husky

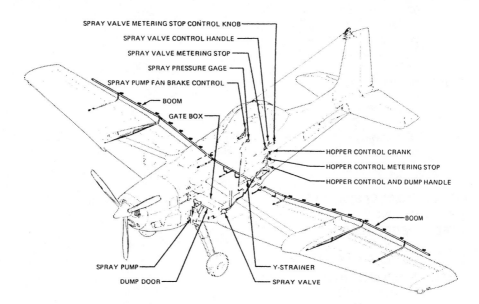

SPRAY VALVE METERING STOP CONTROL KNOB
SPRAY VALVE CONTROL HANDLE
SPRAY VALVE METERING STOP
SPRAY PRESSURE GAGE
SPRAY PUMP FAN BRAKE CONTROL
BOOM
GATE BOX
HOPPER CONTROL CRANK
HOPPER CONTROL METERING STOP
HOPPER CONTROL AND DUMP HANDLE
BOOM
SPRAY PUMP
Y-STRAINER
DUMP DOOR
SPRAY VALVE

Ag Husky liquid dispersal system

agcraft for a wide range of liquid dispersal tasks. With spray booms removed, the AGcarryall may be quickly converted to a six-place intercity transport or an efficient cargo hauler. The AGcarryall factory list price was at one time $36,075.

The Ag Husky turbocharged agricultural aircraft is a restricted category aircraft with its 4,400-pound gross weight.

The 1981 AGwagon and the AGtruck, both of which could have been equipped with a night operations package, were priced at $71,200 and $62,500 repectively. These were available on the 1992 used market for about $53,500 and $47,500. The 1983 AGtruck and Ag Husky (T188C) were $91,400 and $102,600, and in 1992 are valued at about $71,000 and $77,000, respectively.

Table 12-1. AG Carryall performance & specifications.

SPEED:

	Maximum at Sea Level	148 mph	238 kph
	Cruise, 75% Power at 7500 feet	140 mph	225 kph

With spray booms removed, top speed and cruise speed are increased by 10 mph

CRUISE: Recommended Lean Mixture with fuel allowance for engine start, taxi, takeoff, climb and 45 minutes reserve at 45% power

75% Power at 7500 Ft with	Range	395 mi	636 km
55 Gallons Usable Fuel	Time	2.9 hr	2.9 hr
75% Power at 7500 Ft with	Range	565 mi	909 km
74 Gallons Usable Fuel	Time	4.1 hr	4.1 hr

RATE OF CLIMB AT SEA LEVEL	845 fpm	257 mpm
SERVICE CEILING	13,400 ft	4085 m

TAKEOFF PERFORMANCE:

	Ground Roll	885 ft	270 m
	Total Distance Over 50-Ft Obstacle	1450 ft	442 m

LANDING PERFORMANCE:

	Ground Roll	480 ft	146 m
	Total Distance Over 50-Ft Obstacle	1400 ft	427 m

STALL SPEED, (CAS):

	Flaps Up, Power Off	65 mph	105 kph
	Flaps Down, Power Off	56 mph	90 kph

MAXIMUM WEIGHT:

	Normal Category	3350 lb	1519 kg
	Restricted Category	3350 lb	1519 kg

STANDARD EMPTY WEIGHT	1902 lb	863 kg
SPRAY TANK CAPACITY	151 gal	572 liters
WING LOADING	19.3 lb/sq ft	94.2 kg/sq m
POWER LOADING	11.2 lb/hp	5.1 kg/hp
WING SPAN	35 ft, 10 in	10.92 m
WING AREA	174 sq ft	16.2 sq m
LENGTH	25 ft, 9 in	7.85 m
HEIGHT	7 ft, 9 in	2.36 m

FUEL CAPACITY, Total:

	Standard Tanks	61 gal	231 liters
	Long Range Tanks	80 gal	303 liters

OIL CAPACITY	12 qt	11.4 liters

ENGINE: Teledyne Continental IO-520-D Fuel Injection Engine
300 BHP at 2850 RPM (Takeoff)
285 BHP at 2700 RPM (Maximum Continuous)

PROPELLER: Constant Speed, 2 Blades, 82 Inch Diameter (2.08 m)

Table 12-2. AG Wagon and AG Truck performance & specifications.

	No Dispersal Equipment AGwagon		With Liquid Dispersal Equipment Installed AGtruck	
SPEED:				
Maximum at Sea Level	151 mph	240 kph	121 mph	195 kph
Cruise, 75% Power at 6500 Ft	140 mph	225 kph	113 mph	182 kph
CRUISE: *Recommended Lean Mixture with fuel allowance for engine start, taxi, takeoff, climb and 45 minutes reserve at 45% power*				
75% Power at 6500 Ft with Range	230 mi	370 km	180 mi	290 km
36.5 Gallons Usable Fuel Time	1.7 hr	1.7 hr	1.7 hr	1.7 hr
75% Power at 6500 Ft with Range	370 mi	595 km	295 mi	475 km
52 Gallons Usable Fuel** Time	2.7 hr	2.7 hr	2.6 hr	2.6 hr
RATE OF CLIMB AT SEA LEVEL	940 fpm	285 mpm	690 fpm	210 mpm
SERVICE CEILING	15,700 ft	4785 m	11,100 ft	3383 m
TAKEOFF PERFORMANCE:				
Ground Roll	610 ft	186 m	680 ft	207 m
Total Distance Over 50-Ft Obstacle	970 ft	296 m	1090 ft	332 m
LANDING PERFORMANCE:				
Ground Roll	420 ft	128 m	420 ft	128 m
Total Distance Over 50-Ft Obstacle	1265 ft	386 m	1265 ft	386 m
STALL SPEED, (CAS):				
Flaps Up, Power Off	61 mph	98 kph	61 mph	98 kph
Flaps Down, Power Off	57 mph	92 kph	57 mph	92 kph
MAXIMUM WEIGHT:				
Normal Category 3300 lb	1497 kg	3300 lb	1497 kg	
Restricted Category	4000 lb	1814 kg	4200 lb	1905 kg
STANDARD EMPTY WEIGHT:				
With No Dispersal Equipment	1985 lb	900 kg	2059 lb	934 g
With Liquid Dispersal System	2140 lb	971 kg	2214 lb	1004 kg
HOPPER CAPACITY	200 gal	757 liters	280 gal	1060 liters
	27 cu ft	0.75 cu m	37.4 cu ft	1.06 cu m
WING LOADING: *3300 lbs*	16.3 lbs/sq ft	79.8 kg/sq m	16.1 lb/sq ft	78.8 kg/sq m
POWER LOADING: *3300 lbs*	11.0 lbs/hp	5.0 kg/hp	11.0 lb/hp	5.0 kg/hp
WING SPAN	40 ft, 8½ in	12.4 m	41 ft, 8 in	12.7 m
WING AREA	202 sq ft	18.8 sq m	205 sq ft	19.0 sq m
LENGTH	26 ft, 3 in	8.0 m	26 ft, 3 in	8.0 m
HEIGHT	8 ft	2.44 m	8 ft	2.44 m
FUEL CAPACITY, *Total:*				
Standard Tanks	37 gal	140 liters	54 gal	204 liters
Optional Tank	54 gal	204 liters	—	—
OIL CAPACITY	12 qt	11.4 liters	12 qt	11.4 liters

Table 12-2. Continued.

ENGINE: *Teledyne Continental IO-520-D Fuel Injection Engine*

  300 BHP at 2850 RPM (Takeoff) 285 BHP at 2700 RPM (Max. Cont.)

PROPELLER: *Constant Speed, 2 Blades, 82 Inch Diameter (2.08 m)*

**Standard on AGTruck, optional on AGwagon

Table 12-3. 1979 Ag Husky performance & specifications.

Liquid dispersal equipment installed

SPEED:		
Maximum at Sea Level		130 mph
Cruise, 75% Power at 6500 Ft		122 mph

CRUISE: *Recommended lean mixture with fuel allowance for engine start, taxi, takeoff, climb and 45 minutes reserve at 55% power.*

75% Power at 6500 Ft	Range	245 miles
52 Gallons Usable Fuel	Time	2.0 hrs
RATE OF CLIMB AT SEA LEVEL		510 fpm
CERTIFICATED MAXIMUM OPERATING ALTITUDE		14,000 ft
TAKEOFF PERFORMANCE:		
Ground Roll		1290 ft
Total Distance Over 50-Ft Obstacle		2060 ft
LANDING PERFORMANCE:		
Ground Roll		420 ft
Total Distance Over 50-Ft Obstacle		1265 ft
STALL SPEED (CAS):		
Flaps Up, Power Off		71 mph
Flaps Down, Power Off		67 mph
MAXIMUM WEIGHT: Restricted Category		
Takeoff		4400 lbs
Landing		3300 lbs
STANDARD EMPTY WEIGHT		2293 lbs
HOPPER CAPACITY:		
Gallons		280
Cubic Feet		37.4
WING LOADING: Pounds/Sq Ft		21.5
POWER LOADING: Pounds/HP		14.2
FUEL CAPACITY: Total		54 gal
OIL CAPACITY		12 qts
ENGINE: Teledyne Continental, Turbocharged Fuel Injection		TSIO-520-T
310 BHP at 2700 RPM (Maximum Continuous Rating)		
PROPELLER: Type and Diameter		
Constant Speed, 3-Bladed		80 in

13

Caravans

CESSNA QUIT the piston single-engine aircraft business in 1986. That is not to say, however, that the company is out of the prop plane business. At the end of 1982, the Caravan single-engine turboprop appeared. In 1985, it went into production and Cessna continues to make Caravan models to this day.

Although driven by a 600-hp Pratt & Whitney turbo engine, the Caravan shares lots of features with its piston-powered brethren. It looks a lot like a stretched Stationair, with twice the seating capacity. The first Caravan, Caravan I, was designed as a freight carrier with a cargo capacity of 3,500 pounds (3,777 pounds useful load), but it can carry up to 14 passengers. Its model designation is 208A. The windowless cargo carrying configuration was called the Cargomaster.

SUPER CARGOMASTER

A stretched version of the Caravan I was introduced in 1986 as the Super Cargomaster. This model has four feet more of fuselage room and offers a carrying capacity of 4,273 pounds. It features a 675-hp turbo engine and a number of minor changes in ailerons, rudder, and stabilizer to accommodate the added length. This is the 208B. The Caravan also has a floatplane and amphibious floatplane configuration, and a "special missions" package based on a military model. The Grand Caravan was announced in 1990 as a passenger version of the stretched model.

Since the Caravan rolled out in 1985, Cessna has been selling between 60 and 90 per year at approximately $600,000 for a standard model. One of the most important customers is Federal Express, which can't seem to get enough of them.

Performance for takeoffs and landings is close to that of smaller lightplanes, while cruising performance resembles that of the light twins that dominate the Caravan's intended market. Because of its hefty turbo engine, though, the Caravan cruises at more than 180 knots, and has a service ceiling of up to 25,500 ft. That doesn't match jet performance by any means, but it is enough to get you where you're going.

Doug Rotondi, director of training and flight standards for Corporate Air, in Billings, Montana, is an experienced Caravan pilot, complementing approxi-

Federal Express Caravans

mately 12,800 hours total time. His company flies for Federal Express, running Caravans all over the country.

PILOT'S POINTS

"The control feel and pressures are a lot like a 182," he said. "The Caravan has excellent power. At full weight, the ride is comparable to 1 person with 1 hour's fuel in a 210. Without the pod, it does even better.

"The Caravan does a fine job. It's been bad mouthed recently for performance in ice, but we haven't seen it. Actually, I think it's not a bad airplane in ice. We do a lot of flying in mountain regions, where icing conditions are frequently encountered, and we've found that it doesn't handle badly at all.

"I like the way that the Caravan flies, and we are impressed by its performance. It outperforms the book if you set it up properly. It isn't the most comfortable aircraft in the world; it keeps the pilot awake, but long hauls can be a bit rough."

Cessna is stressing the adaptability of the Caravan models, and that has always been the company's strong suit. The roles that Cessna views for the Caravan include corporate or personal transport, military surveillance, fire fighting, medevac, and skydiving.

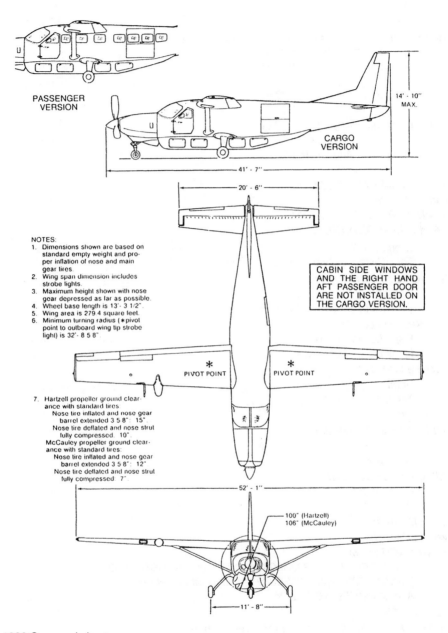

PASSENGER
VERSION

14' - 10"
MAX.

CARGO
VERSION

41' - 7"

20' - 6"

NOTES:
1. Dimensions shown are based on standard empty weight and proper inflation of nose and main gear tires.
2. Wing span dimension includes strobe lights.
3. Maximum height shown with nose gear depressed as far as possible.
4. Wheel base length is 13'- 3 1/2".
5. Wing area is 279.4 square feet.
6. Minimum turning radius (✱pivot point to outboard wing tip strobe light) is 32'- 8 5 8"

CABIN SIDE WINDOWS AND THE RIGHT HAND AFT PASSENGER DOOR ARE NOT INSTALLED ON THE CARGO VERSION.

✱
PIVOT POINT

✱
PIVOT POINT

7. Hartzell propeller ground clearance with standard tires:
    Nose tire inflated and nose gear barrel extended 3 5 8": 15".
    Nose tire deflated and nose strut fully compressed: 10".
    McCauley propeller ground clearance with standard tires:
    Nose tire inflated and nose gear barrel extended 3 5 8": 12".
    Nose tire deflated and nose strut fully compressed: 7".

52' - 1"

100" (Hartzell)
106" (McCauley)

11' - 8"

1990 Caravan I views

Table 13-1. 1990 Caravan I performance & specifications.

SPEED:

Maximum Cruise at 10,000 Ft	171 knots
Maximum Cruise at 20,000 Ft	159 knots

RANGE: With 2224 pounds usable fuel and fuel allowance for engine start, taxi, takeoff, climb, descent and 45 minutes reserve.

Maximum Cruise at 10,000 Ft	888 nm
	5.4 hrs
Maximum Cruise at 18,000 Ft	1062 nm
	6.9 hrs
Maximum Range at 10,000 Ft	962 nm
	6.4 hrs
Maximum Range at 18,000 Ft	1079 nm
	7.2 hrs

RATE OF CLIMB AT SEA LEVEL	770 fpm
SERVICE CEILING	21,900 ft
MAXIMUM OPERATING ALTITUDE	25,000 ft

TAKEOFF PERFORMANCE:

Ground Roll	1575 ft
Total Distance Over 50-Ft Obstacle	2840 ft

LANDING PERFORMANCE:

Ground Roll	915 ft
Total Distance Over 50-Ft Obstacle	1740 ft

STALL SPEED (KCAS):

Flaps Up, Idle Power	78 knots
Flaps Down, Idle Power	61 knots

MAXIMUM WEIGHT:

Ramp	8785 lbs
Takeoff	8750 lbs
Landing	8500 lbs

STANDARD EMPTY WEIGHT:

Cargo Version	3997 lbs
Passenger Version	4103 lbs

MAXIMUM USEFUL LOAD:

Cargo Version	4788 lbs
Passenger Version	4682 lbs

WING LOADING:	31.3 lbs/sq ft
POWER LOADING:	14.6 lbs/shp

FUEL CAPACITY: Total

S/N 208B0001 Thru 208B0089 Not Modified with SK208-52	335 gal
S/N 208B0001 Thru 208B0089 Modified with SK208-52	
And S/N 208B0090 And On	335.6 gal

OIL CAPACITY	14 qts

ENGINE: Pratt & Whitney Canada Inc. Free Turbine

Flat Rated at 600 Shaft Horsepower	PT6A-114

PROPELLER: Hartzell 3-Bladed, Constant Speed, Full

Feathering, Reversible. Diameter	100 in
McCauley 3-Bladed, Constant Speed, Full Feathering, Reversible. Diameter	106 in

14

Buying a used Cessna

IF YOU BUY A CESSNA LIGHTPLANE, you are, by definition, buying a used aircraft. This introduces some special factors in making your purchase. While new aircraft can be purchased from a retailer at a set price, and are expected to be up to spec, used aircraft can be purchased from a variety of sources, are subject to considerations of wear, and are priced according to a wide variety of factors.

While it is not the intention of this book to provide a complete purchasing guide, we offer here a few suggestions to point you in the right direction.

The first problem you will be faced with is selecting an appropriate aircraft type. Here, you need to balance your flying needs against available finances. Newer and larger models are more expensive than older, smaller models. Some models hold their value very well; others less so because the model is unpopular or has undesirable features. Then, of course, there is the matter of taste.

START LOOKING

Once you have selected a model or set of models to pursue, and a price range, the search may begin. Here, there are a variety of sources, ranging from the airport bulletin board to *Trade-a-Plane*, based in Crossville, Tennessee, which is probably the number one source for national ads, but there are also several other advertising publications. You will also find ads in regional aviation publications and you should not omit the local newspaper, especially the Sunday edition of a paper in the closest large metropolitan area. A shopper with a computer and a modem could log on to several computer bulletin boards offering aircraft ads.

When you have found several aircraft of interest, you need to take a look at them. Again, this is often more difficult than simply flying out to the regional dealer. You might save yourself a lot of work by finding a good used-plane dealer, but you should expect to pay more (although not necessarily much more). If you have to fly out to see the plane, it's generally a good idea to bring along an experienced friend—preferably a mechanic—to doublecheck your observations.

CHECK IT OUT

Next, when you find the right plane, you should put it through an inspection by a mechanic. A dealer or individual might offer a presale check as a standard item; recently, some have shied away from the presale check due to liability concerns. Used aircraft need to have all of the ADs checked for compliance, and there are also various stress points, such as wing attachment points and landing gear, that require special examination. It's a good idea to find a mechanic with a lot of Cessna experience. Luckily, with Cessna's market presence, that isn't very difficult at all.

Next, check out all the papers. Check the logs, and ask questions. Make sure it can pass an annual, which ideally should be a sale contingency.

When you are satisfied that everything is in order and this is the plane you really want, it is time to write out that check and complete your paperwork. Make sure you get title insurance because the past history of an aircraft can be complicated; for example, was it ever used as collateral for a loan?

ENJOYING OWNERSHIP

A number of publications and general-interest airplane books provide specific information and general information on purchasing a used aircraft. The FAA offers a pamphlet entitled *Plane Sense*, which contains general purchase and ownership information including an outline of all the paperwork you need to do.

Cessna publishes information on used airplane purchases in its manual supplements. Take note of the "Airworthiness of Older Airplanes" heading, in the "Deferred Maintenance" section. This contains useful tips on inspection points and also reminds you that the initial low cost of a used aircraft is partially offset by the subsequent higher cost of maintenance. Because Cessna is not producing new airplanes, view this as advice regarding purchase of older versus new aircraft.

Cessna Aircraft Company has granted permission to present noteworthy inspection points:

- Wing attach points and fuselage carry-through structure.
- Wing spar capstrips, especially the lower ones.
- Horizontal and vertical stabilizer attach points and spar structure.
- Control surface structure and attach points.
- Engine mounts and cowlings.
- Landing gear structure and attach points.
- Structural and flooring integrity of seat and equipment attachments.
- Pressurized structures, especially around all doors, windows, windshields and other cutouts on pressurized airplanes.

Additional information is available from general interest and special interest groups (chapter 15): Aircraft Owners and Pilots Association (AOPA), the Cessna Owner Organization, Cessna Pilots Association, and others.

15

Cessna organizations

Aircraft organizations have a habit of emerging, merging, and disappearing. This list is only a starting point. Watch for club advertisements in publications such as *Pacific Flyer*, *General Aviation News and Flyer*, *Private Pilot*, *FLYING*, *AOPA Pilot*, and the like. Ask around the airport to see if someone belongs to a club. Sift through the stack of publications in a pilot lounge and perhaps you'll find a copy of one of the newsletters.

Cardinal Club
1701 Saint Andrew's Drive
Lawrence, KS 66047

The Cardinal Club is an organization of 1,200 devoted Cessna Cardinal fans. You do not have to have your own aircraft to join—just be interested in Cardinals. The Cardinal Club provides support for airframe improvements and mods, and provides free advertising for members.

Cessna 150/152 Club
P.O. Box 15388
Durham, NC 27704

The Cessna 150/152 club is devoted to the support of Cessna's popular trainer line, publishing a newsletter and keeping members abreast of maintenance issues.

Cessna Owner Organization
P.O. Box 337
Iola, WI 54945

The Cessna Owner Organization was formed when the Skyhawk and Skylane Clubs merged. This group has several thousand members and publishes the *Cessna Owner Magazine*. Its mission is to provide information and assistance to keep Cessnas flying.

Cessna Pilots Association
Wichita Airport
2120 Airport Road, P.O. Box 12948
Wichita, KS 67277

The Cessna Pilots Association calls itself the largest "type" club in the world, serving 14,000 members. It publishes a magazine, maintains a complete technical library on all Cessna aircraft, provides general assistance, and provides maintenance information.

International Bird Dog Association
3939 San Pedro, N.E., Suite C-8
Albuquerque, NM 87110

This type club supports the military Cessna L-19, popularly known as the Bird Dog. It maintains registration files of Bird Dog serial numbers and provides maintenance and ownership information.

International Cessna 120/140 Association
P.O. Box 830092
Richardson, TX 75083

The Cessna 120/140 Association provides information on and support for 120s and 140s. The group has about 1,500 members and publishes a regular newsletter.

National 210 Owners' Association
P.O. Box 1065
La Canada Flintridge, CA 91011

The club publishes the *National 210 Air Letter,* a newsletter for its membership.

International Cessna 170 Association
P.O. Box 1667
Lebanon, MO 65536

International 180/185 Club
P.O. Box 222
Georgetown, TX 78626

International 195 Club
P.O. Box 737
Merced, CA 95340

16

Further reading

OTHER BOOKS ABOUT CESSNA AIRPLANES might provide additional information for the Cessna owner or prospective owner.

The Cessna 150 and 152 by Bill Clarke; TAB Books, Blue Ridge Summit, Pennsylvania; 2nd edition scheduled for publication in 1993.

The Cessna 172 by Bill Clarke; TAB Books, Blue Ridge Summit, Pennsylvania; 2nd edition scheduled for publication in 1993.

Cessna, Wings for the World: The Single-Engine Development Story by William D. Thompson; 1991, William D. Thompson, printed by Maverick Publications, Inc., Bend, Oregon.

Cessna, A Master's Expression by Edward H. Phillips; 1985, Flying Books, Eagan, Minnesota.

Wings of Cessna, Model 120 to the Citation III by Edward H. Phillips; 1986, Flying Books, Eagan, Minnesota.

Tips on Buying Cessna Singles by Alton K. Marsh; 1990, Alton K. Marsh, printed by Aviation Book Co., Santa Clarita, California.

Spotter's guide

Cessna L19 Bird Dog. Small military Cessna, notable for its high stance (note lower body curve) and heavy construction.

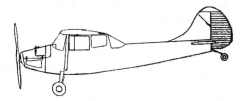

Cessna 120 and 140. Small, two-place, older taildraggers. The 120s do not have the triangular rear window and are distinguished by not having flaps or electrical system, though often retrofitted. Early versions had fabric wings.

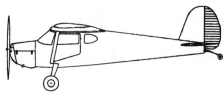

Cessna 190 and 195 (Military versions LC-126A, LC-126B, LC-126C). Large taildragger distinguished by big radial engine (Continental 190 or Jacobs 195), unique shape, and narrow window arrangement.

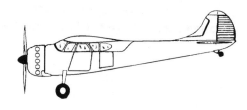

Cessna 170. Medium-size, four-place, taildragger, forerunner of the 172. Early versions had fabric wing and lacked the dorsal fin extension on the tail.

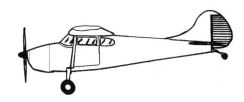

Cessna 180, Skywagon, Skywagon II.
Medium-large taildragger. Heavier than the 170, with additional window, baggage compartment, and optional bubble window in door.

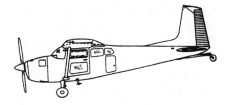

Cessna 185 (Military versions U-17A, U-17B). Essentially the same airframe as the 180, with internal bracing and some wing modifications. Distinguish from 180 by the large dorsal fin. Available in an agricultural version as the AGcarryall.

Cessna 172, Skyhawk, Skyhawk II, Hawk XP, 172 Powermatic, 175, Skylark, Cutlass (Military versions T-41A, T-41B Mescalero, T-41C, T-41D). The classic Cessna four-place airplane. Variations over the years have included rear window (wraparound in later versions), tail modifications, and wings. The basic shape has remained the same. The 175 and Skylark have cowl flaps.

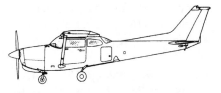

Cessna 172RG, Cutlass RG. A high-performance 172 variant with retractable gear. Same basic 172 airframe.

Cessna 177 Cardinal (Classic). Note the trim shape, heavily sloped windshield, and elongated "sports car" appearance.

Cessna 177RG, Cardinal RG. A Cardinal with retractable gear.

Cessna 150. Cessna's two-place trainer. Distinguish by size from the Skyhawk; distinguish from the 152 by slightly stubbier appearance (smaller engine compartment). Hard to tell a well-kept 150 from a 152 at a glance. Early 150s (pre-1966) have a square tail; late 150s have wraparound rear window (shown).

Cessna 152. The 100-octane version of the 150. Slightly longer, slightly larger engine compartment.

Cessna 182, Skylane, and Turbo Skylane. Midsized workhorse aircraft. Distinguish from the Skyhawk by heavier construction, slight size difference, and extended cabin area. Also available in retractable versions as the Skylane RG and Turbo Skylane RG.

Cessna 205, 206, Skywagon 206, Turbo Super Skywagon, Super Skywagon, Turbo Skywagon, Stationair 6. These large single-engine aircraft use the same basic airframe. Distinguish by its size, three-blade prop, and three windows on each side.

Cessna 207, Skywagon 207, Turbo Skywagon 207, Stationair 7, Stationair 8. A "stretched" 206. Similar airframe, but longer. Additional side window brings the total to four on each side.

Cessna 210 Centurion, Turbo Centurion, Centurion II, Pressurized Centurion. Somewhat heavier than the Skywagon. Centurion has no wing struts, a three-blade prop, and larger cowling. Wing angle has varied by model year. Newer airplanes have a single rear window; older airplanes have a centerpost between rear windows.

Cessna AGwagon, AGtruck, 188A, 188B.
These models share the basic agricultural
plane airframe. Difference is in engine
power, but the cowling is the same.

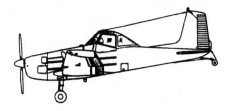

Cessna AGcarryall. Airframe is the Cessna
185, with lower pod, cable deflector,
square tail, spray equipment, and
conventional gear (taildragger).

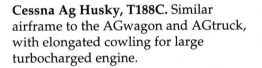

Cessna Ag Husky, T188C. Similar
airframe to the AGwagon and AGtruck,
with elongated cowling for large
turbocharged engine.

**Cessna 208, Cessna Caravan, Grand
Caravan, Cargomaster, Super
Cargomaster (Military version U-27A).**
The largest prop-driven single-engine
Cessna. Passenger version (Caravan)
looks like a stretched 207. Cargomaster
freight version is shown. The Grand
Caravan has a stretched airframe.

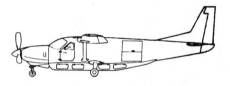

Size comparison between a Cessna 152 and
the Caravan, demonstrating the dramatic
size difference between the smallest and
largest of Cessna's single-engine line.

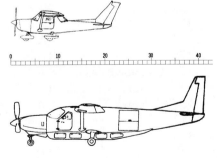

Prices

CURRENT USED PRICES of selected Cessna aircraft, by year of manufacture. Note that these are averages, and actual sale prices vary widely according to condition (particularly with older aircraft). This information is provided courtesy of the *Aircraft Bluebook Price Digest* (Copyright 1991, Intertec Publishing, Overland Park, Kansas).

Model	Year	Price	Year	Price
208 Caravan	1991(new)	944,700	1985	710,000
Pressurized 210	1986	280,000	1978	86,000
210	1986	185,000	1970	41,000
207	1984	142,000	1970	46,000
206	1986	171,000	1970	46,500
205	1964	32,000		
195	1952	37,000		
A188 (Truck)	1983	71,500	1970	21,500
T188C (Husky)	1983	77,500		
185	1985	114,000	1970	41,500
182RG	1986	127,500	1978	55,500
182	1986	108,000	1970	34,000
180	1981	64,000	1970	35,000
177RG	1978	40,500	1971	28,500
177	1978	38,000	1970	23,500
175	1960	14,000		
172RG (Cutlass RG II)	1984	63,000		
172Q (Cutlass II)	1984	56,000		
R172K (Hawk XP)	1981	44,500		
172	1986	71,000	1970	21,250
170	1956	20,000		
152	1985	40,500	1978	24,000
150	1977	16,000	1966	10,000
140	1949	10,000		

CHARTS

The figures below show the trends in new and used airplane prices for 150s and 152s. The dramatic price changes demonstrate the industry's current marketing problems.

New 150/152 Prices

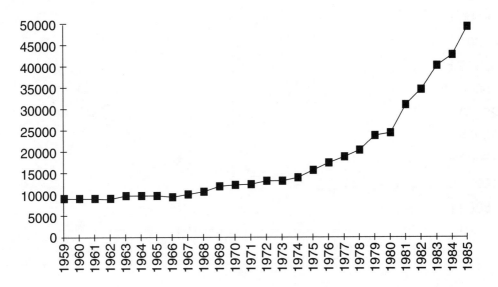

Used 150/152 Prices
Year of manufacture versus current selling prices.

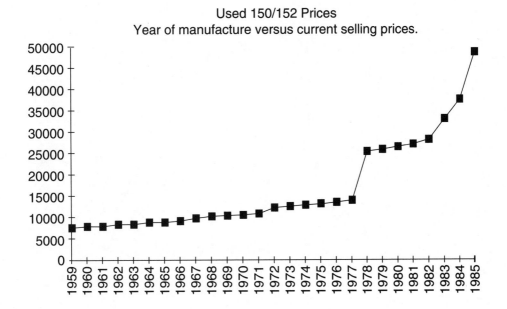

The 152 was introduced in 1978; note the immediate jump in pricing. (Used airplane prices are represented by the white boxes.) The stability of early years contrasts markedly with post 1978 prices, which are characterized by large price jumps. Demand has remained strong for late model used planes, as seen by the close match between today's values of used aircraft.

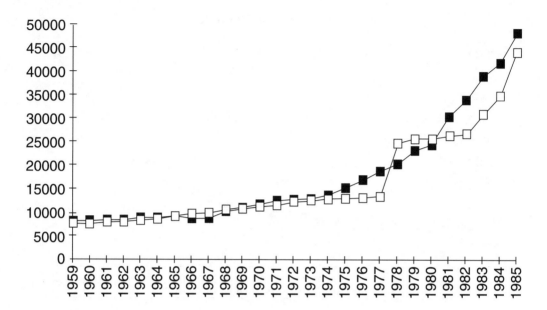

Sales

A COMPLETE TABULATION of Cessna single-engine sales begins on page 124.

SALES. Cessna commercial aircraft sales through December 1990.

This table provides Cessna's per-year sales figures to all distributors including direct sales.

Model	1951	1952	1953	1954	1955	1956	1957	1958	1959
120	-	-	-	-	-	-	-	-	-
140	38	-	2	-	-	-	-	-	-
190	28	26	7	-	-	-	-	-	-
195	69	161	116	44	16	6	1	-	-
170	416	1186	663	495	448	72	36	-	-
175/Skylark	-	-	-	-	-	-	-	702	727
205	-	-	-	-	-	-	-	-	-
150/A150	-	-	-	-	-	-	-	122	648
F150/FRA150 (Reims Aviation)	-	-	-	-	-	-	-	-	-
152/A152	-	-	-	-	-	-	-	-	-
F152/FRA152 (Reims Aviation)	-	-	-	-	-	-	-	-	-
172/Skyhawk	-	-	-	-	173	1419	939	790	874
F172/Skyhawk (Reims Aviation)	-	-	-	-	-	-	-	-	-
Cutlass	-	-	-	-	-	-	-	-	-
Hawk XP	-	-	-	-	-	-	-	-	-
Reims Hawk XP	-	-	-	-	-	-	-	-	-
177/Cardinal	-	-	-	-	-	-	-	-	-
Reims Rocket	-	-	-	-	-	-	-	-	-
Cardinal RG	-	-	-	-	-	-	-	-	-
Reims Cardinal RG	-	-	-	-	-	-	-	-	-
Cutlass RG	-	-	-	-	-	-	-	-	-
182/Skylane	-	-	-	-	-	983	835	874	774
Reims 182/Skylane	-	-	-	-	-	-	-	-	-
182/Skylane RG	-	-	-	-	-	-	-	-	-
Reims 182/Skylane RG	-	-	-	-	-	-	-	-	-
Skywagon 180	-	-	664	646	880	530	438	262	258
Skywagon 185	-	-	-	-	-	-	-	-	-
Ag Wagon	-	-	-	-	-	-	-	-	-
Ag Carryall	-	-	-	-	-	-	-	-	-
Ag Pickup	-	-	-	-	-	-	-	-	-
Ag Truck	-	-	-	-	-	-	-	-	-
Ag Husky	-	-	-	-	-	-	-	-	-
Super Skylane 206	-	-	-	-	-	-	-	-	-
Skywagon 206	-	-	-	-	-	-	-	-	-
Stationair 206	-	-	-	-	-	-	-	-	-
Stationair 6	-	-	-	-	-	-	-	-	-
Skywagon 207	-	-	-	-	-	-	-	-	-
Stationair 7	-	-	-	-	-	-	-	-	-
Stationair 8	-	-	-	-	-	-	-	-	-
210/Centurion	-	-	-	-	-	-	-	-	-
Pressurized 210/Centurion	-	-	-	-	-	-	-	-	-
208 Caravan I	-	-	-	-	-	-	-	-	-

1960	1961	1962	1963	1964	1965	1966	1967	1968	1969	1970	1971
-	-	-	-	-	-	-	-	-	-	-	-
-	-	-	-	-	-	-	-	-	-	-	-
-	-	-	-	-	-	-	-	-	-	-	-
-	-	-	-	-	-	-	-	-	-	-	-
-	-	-	-	-	-	-	-	-	-	-	-
501	126	50	13	-	-	-	-	-	-	-	-
-	-	165	353	55	1	-	-	-	-	-	-
354	344	331	472	804	1637	3087	2114	2007	1714	832	879
-	-	-	-	-	-	100	150	152	136	169	150
-	-	-	-	-	-	-	-	-	-	-	-
-	-	-	-	-	-	-	-	-	-	-	-
1015	903	889	1146	1401	1436	1597	839	1206	1170	759	827
-	-	-	-	-	114	108	142	103	84	63	83
-	-	-	-	-	-	-	-	-	-	-	-
-	-	-	-	-	-	-	-	-	-	-	-
-	-	-	-	-	-	-	-	-	-	-	-
-	-	-	-	-	-	-	557	601	255	160	109
-	-	-	-	-	-	-	1	65	81	65	67
-	-	-	-	-	-	-	-	-	-	17	128
-	-	-	-	-	-	-	-	-	-	-	29
-	-	-	-	-	-	-	-	-	-	-	-
667	575	824	642	778	865	993	836	778	673	371	468
-	-	-	-	-	-	-	-	-	-	-	-
-	-	-	-	-	-	-	-	-	-	-	-
283	130	114	128	146	157	164	87	97	110	68	56
-	293	229	94	82	98	121	112	116	141	111	107
-	-	-	-	-	-	193	95	143	141	118	140
-	-	-	-	-	-	-	-	-	-	-	-
-	-	-	-	-	-	-	-	-	-	-	-
-	-	-	-	-	-	-	-	-	-	-	-
-	-	-	-	-	-	-	-	-	-	-	-
-	-	-	-	41	126	161	106	88	60	53	8
-	-	-	61	240	181	252	243	229	207	145	20
-	-	-	-	-	-	-	-	-	-	5	129
-	-	-	-	-	-	-	-	-	-	-	-
-	-	-	-	-	-	-	-	-	123	47	37
-	-	-	-	-	-	-	-	-	-	-	-
-	-	-	-	-	-	-	-	-	-	-	-
610	171	281	156	283	224	257	226	190	181	188	171
-	-	-	-	-	-	-	-	-	-	-	-
-	-	-	-	-	-	-	-	-	-	-	-

Continued fron page 125.

Model	1972	1973	1974	1975	1976	1977	1978	1979	1980
120	-	-	-	-	-	-	-	-	-
140	-	-	-	-	-	-	-	-	-
190	-	-	-	-	-	-	-	-	-
195	-	-	-	-	-	-	-	-	-
170	-	-	-	-	-	-	-	-	-
175/Skylark	-	-	-	-	-	-	-	-	-
205	-	-	-	-	-	-	-	-	-
150/A150	1100	1460	1080	1269	1399	429	-	-	-
F150/FRA150 (Reims Aviation)	170	214	144	132	129	108	4	-	-
152/A152	-	-	-	-	-	1522	1918	1268	887
F152/FRA152 (Reims Aviation)	-	-	-	-	-	19	110	142	142
172/Skyhawk	984	1550	1786	1885	1896	1711	1810	1621	1022
F172/Skyhawk (Reims Aviation)	97	139	158	143	151	151	123	144	137
Cutlass	-	-	-	-	-	-	-	-	-
Hawk XP	-	-	-	-	189	598	213	254	155
Reims Hawk XP	-	-	-	-	1	27	15	24	8
177/Cardinal	145	212	167	169	183	122	69	1	-
Reims Rocket	78	81	74	39	21	19	-	-	-
Cardinal RG	101	126	194	186	277	189	96	-	-
Reims Cardinal RG	32	23	30	20	19	19	4	-	-
Cutlass RG	-	-	-	-	-	-	-	185	186
182/Skylane	696	1061	814	945	879	826	596	660	425
Reims 182/Skylane	-	-	-	-	21	39	34	35	29
182/Skylane RG	-	-	-	-	-	82	660	558	340
Reims 182/Skylane RG	-	-	-	-	-	-	18	23	13
Skywagon 180	72	104	114	123	131	123	117	108	51
Skywagon 185	131	193	262	261	289	264	226	242	200
Ag Wagon	182	169	155	75	51	36	33	35	15
Ag Carryall	8	8	17	29	18	12	3	13	2
Ag Pickup	22	15	7	9	-	-	-	-	-
Ag Truck	42	157	350	388	333	269	152	89	63
Ag Husky	-	-	-	-	-	-	27	114	110
Super Skylane 206	-	-	-	-	-	-	-	-	-
Skywagon 206	-	-	-	-	-	-	-	-	-
Stationair 206	203	310	389	467	497	480	-	-	-
Stationair 6	-	-	-	-	-	101	560	714	559
Skywagon 207	12	15	43	42	50	48	-	-	-
Stationair 7	-	-	-	-	-	6	75	66	1
Stationair 8	-	-	-	-	-	-	-	10	95
210/Centurion	220	351	474	531	520	719	710	688	437
Pressurized 210/Centurion	-	-	-	-	-	-	158	261	192
208 Caravan I	-	-	-	-	-	-	-	-	-

1981	1982	1983	1984	1985	1986	1987	1988	1989	1990	Total
-	-	-	-	-	-	-	-	-	-	2,171*
-	-	-	-	-	-	-	-	-	-	5,430*
-	-	-	-	-	-	-	-	-	-	230*
-	-	-	-	-	-	-	-	-	-	866*
-	-	-	-	-	-	-	-	-	-	5,173*
-	-	-	-	-	-	-	-	-	-	2,119
-	-	-	-	-	-	-	-	-	-	574
-	-	-	-	-	-	-	-	-	-	22,082
-	-	-	-	-	-	-	-	-	-	1,758
634	265	167	86	113	-	-	-	-	-	6,860
79	52	20	9	16	33	18	-	-	-	640
939	319	231	187	194	115	-	-	-	-	33,629
83	62	19	20	5	14	1	-	-	-	2,144
-	8	20	8	-	-	-	-	-	-	36
40	3	-	-	-	-	-	-	-	-	1,452
5	5	-	-	-	-	-	-	-	-	85
-	-	-	-	1	-	-	-	-	-	2,751
-	-	-	-	-	-	-	-	-	-	591
-	-	-	-	-	-	-	-	-	-	1,314
-	-	-	-	-	-	-	-	-	-	176
271	107	54	40	15	1	-	-	-	-	1,159
294	196	101	85	90	39	-	-	-	-	19,643
11	-	-	-	-	-	-	-	-	-	169
156	90	50	51	31	11	-	-	-	-	2,029
19	-	-	-	-	-	-	-	-	-	73
31	1	-	-	-	-	-	-	-	-	6,193
156	65	26	22	18	-	-	-	-	-	3,859
8	-	-	-	-	-	-	-	-	-	1,589
-	-	-	-	-	-	-	-	-	-	110
-	-	-	-	-	-	-	-	-	-	53
49	32	20	5	-	-	-	-	-	-	1,949
80	37	16	1	1	-	-	-	-	-	386
-	-	-	-	-	-	-	-	-	-	643
-	-	-	-	-	-	-	-	-	-	1,578
-	-	-	-	-	-	-	-	-	-	2,480
451	188	116	96	70	94	2	-	-	-	2,951
-	-	-	-	-	-	-	-	-	-	417
-	-	-	-	-	-	-	-	-	-	148
54	33	14	19	-	-	-	-	-	-	225
371	173	71	85	66	53	3	-	-	-	8,453
104	43	35	19	31	8	-	-	-	-	851
-	-	-	-	63	53	77	90	89	66	438

*Total includes aircraft built before 1951.

Index

Other Bestsellers Of Related Interest

ABCs of SAFE FLYING—3rd Edition
—David Frazier

Take a step-by-step look at operational safety. This book presents a wealth of flight safety information in a fun-to-read format. The author's anecdotal episodes, as well as NTSB accident reports, lend both humor and sobering reality to the text. Detailed photographs, maps, and illustrations ensure you understand key concepts and techniques. 192 pages, illustrated. Book No. 3757, $14.95 paperback only

The classic you've been searching for . . .
STICK AND RUDDER: An Explanation of the Art of Flying—Wolfgang Langewiesche

Students, certified pilots, and instructors alike have praised this book as *"the most useful guide to flying ever written"* The book explains the important phases of the art of flying, in a way the learner can use. It shows precisely what the pilot does when he flies, just how he does it, and why. 400 pages, 88 illustrations. Book No. 3820, $19.95 hardcover only

GENERAL AVIATION LAW
—Jerry A. Eichenberger

Although the regulatory burden that is part of flying sometimes seems overwhelming, it need not take the pleasure out of your flight time. This survey of aviation regulations gives a solid understanding of FAA procedures and functions, airman ratings and maintenance certificates, the implications of aircraft ownership, and more. It allows you to recognize legal problems before they result in FAA investigations and potentially serious consequences. 240 pages. Book No. 3431, $16.95 paperback only

UNDERSTANDING AERONAUTICAL CHARTS—Terry T. Lankford

Filled with practical applications for beginning and veteran pilots, this book will show you how to plan your flights quickly, easily, and accurately. It covers all the charts you'll need for flight planning, including those for VFR, IFR, SID, STAR, Loran, and helicopter flights. As you examine the criteria, purpose, and limitations of each chart, you'll learn the author's proven system for interpreting and using charts. 320 pages, 183 illustrations. Book No. 3844, $17.95 paperback only

THE PILOT'S GUIDE TO WEATHER REPORTS, FORECASTS & FLIGHT PLANNING
—Terry T. Lankford

Don't get caught in weather you're not prepared to handle. Learn how to use today's weather information services with this comprehensive guide. It shows you how to access weather services efficiently, translate briefings correctly, and apply reports and forecasts to specific preflight and in-flight situations to expand your margin of safety. 397 pages, 123 illustrations. Book No. 3582, $19.95 paperback only

AVOIDING COMMON PILOT ERRORS: An Air Traffic Controller's View—John Stewart

This essential reference—written from the controller's perspective—interprets the mistakes pilots often make when operating in controlled airspace. It cites situations frequently encountered by controllers that show how improper training, lack of preflight preparation, poor communication skills, and confusing regulations can lead to pilot mistakes. 240 pages, 32 illustrations. Book No. 2434, $17.95 paperback only

GOOD TAKEOFFS AND GOOD LANDINGS
—2nd Edition—Joe Christy, revised and updated by Ken George

Perform safe, precise takeoffs and landings. This complete guide includes material on obstructions to visibility, wind shear avoidance, unlighted night landings, and density altitude. You'll also find a recap of recent takeoff and landing mishaps and how to avoid them, expanded coverage of FARs, and information on the new recreational license. 208 pages, 76 illustrations. Book No. 3611, $15.95 paperback only

BE A BETTER PILOT: Making the Right
Decisions—Paul A. Craig

Why do good pilots sometimes make bad decisions? This book takes an in-depth look at the ways pilots make important preflight and in-flight decisions. It dispels the myths surrounding the pilot personality, provides straightforward solutions to poor decisionmaking, and determines traits that pilots appear to share—traits that affect the way they approach situations. 240 pages, 76 illustrations. Book No. 3675, $15.95 paperback, $24.95 hardcover

CROSS-COUNTRY FLYING—3rd Edition
—Paul Garrison, Norval Kennedy, and R. Randall Padfield

Establish and maintain sound flying habits with this classic cockpit reference. It includes revised information on Mode-C requirements, direct user access terminal usage (DUAT), LORAN-C navigation, hand-held transceivers, affordable moving maps, and over-water flying techniques. Plus, you'll find expanded coverage of survival equipment, TCSs, fuel management and conservation, mountain flying techniques, and off-airport landings. 328 pages, 148 illustrations. Book No. 3640, $19.95 paperback only

MAKE YOUR AIRPLANE LAST FOREVER
—Nicholas E. Silitch

Even if you're an experienced mechanic, you can extend the operating life of your airplane, increase its safety and dependability, and keep high-priced emergency repairs to a minimum. This book will show you how. It covers the aircraft engine as well as techniques for testing avionics and related equipment. 160 pages, 83 illustrations. Book No. 2328, $13.95 paperback only

Look for These and Other TAB Books at Your Local Bookstore

To Order Call Toll Free 1-800-822-8158
(24-hour telephone service available.)

or write to TAB Books, Blue Ridge Summit, PA 17294-0840.

Title	Product No.	Quantity	Price

☐ Check or money order made payable to TAB Books

Charge my ☐ VISA ☐ MasterCard ☐ American Express

Acct. No. _____ Exp. _____

Signature: _____

Name: _____

Address: _____

City: _____

State: _____ Zip: _____

Subtotal $ _____

Postage and Handling
($3.00 in U.S., $5.00 outside U.S.) $ _____

Add applicable state and local
sales tax $ _____

TOTAL $ _____

TAB Books catalog free with purchase; otherwise send $1.00 in check or money order and receive $1.00 credit on your next purchase.

Orders outside U.S. must pay with international money in U.S. dollars drawn on a U.S. bank.

TAB Guarantee: If for any reason you are not satisfied with the book(s) you order, simply return it (them) within 15 days and receive a full refund.

BC